AN UNCOMMON JOURNEY

AN
UNCOMMON
JOURNEY

From Vienna to Shanghai to America
A Brother and Sister Escape to Freedom During World War II

DEBORAH STROBIN
&
ILIE WACS

---

with SJ Hodges

BARRICADE BOOKS
FORT LEE, NEW JERSEY

Published by Barricade Books Inc.
2037 Lemoine Ave.
Suite 362
Fort Lee, NJ 07024

www.barricadebooks.com

Library of Congress Cataloging-in-Publication Data

Strobin, Deborah, 1936-
 An uncommon journey : from Vienna to Shanghai to America : a brother and sister escape to freedom during World War II / Deborah Strobin & Ilie Wacs with SJ Hodges.
    p. cm.
ISBN 978-1-56980-504-6 (paperback)
ISBN 978-1-56980-452-0 (hardcover)
1. Jews--Austria--Vienna--Biography. 2. Strobin, Deborah, 1936- 3. Wacs, Ilie, 1927- 4. Refugees, Jewish--China--Shanghai--Biography. 5. Refugees, Jewish--United States--Biography. I. Wacs, Ilie, 1927- II. Hodges, S. J. III. Title.
DS135.A93S77 2011
305.892'40730922--dc23
[B]
                            2011027606

FIRST PRINTING IN PAPERBACK

Manufactured in the United States of America

CONTENTS

DEDICATIONS

In memory of my parents, Moritz and Henia Wacs; my late husband, Edward; and dear friend, Donald Fisher. With love to my sons, Mark and Mitchell Strobin, and their wives, Christina and Cynthia; my grandchildren. Alexandra, Georgianna, Alexis, Nicholas, and Samantha.
   —*Deborah Strobin*

In memory of my parents, Moritz and Henia Wacs; my late wife, Sylvia; and Charles Jordan. Great appreciation to my daughters, Maris and Darin; my grandchildren, Jordan, Sydney, Lindsey, Isaac, and Adam.
   —*Ilie Wacs*

ACKNOWLEDGMENTS

Deborah would like to thank Maura Teitelbaum, our agent; Carole Stuart, our publisher; Mitchell Berger, M.D.; the Reverend and Mrs. Warren Debenham; Millard Drexler; Sydnie Kohara; Lois Lehrman; Charles Wilson, M.D.; my sons, Mark and Mitchell.

A special thank you to Bobby Goldman whose encouragement helped start the process that has resulted in this book, and to Susan Hodges, for helping us to make this book a reality.

Ilie would also like to thank Maura Teitelbaum and Carole Stuart. He especially thanks his daughters, Maris and Darin, and his companion, Susan, for all their help and understanding in this endeavor.

PREFACE

During a brief period, 1938-1945, Shanghai was the home of a vibrant community of Jewish refugees, primarily from Nazi Germany and Nazi Austria.

Eighteen thousand of us found a haven there.

Shanghai was the only place in the entire world that accepted refugees without any restrictions. All that was needed was passage on a ship to China.

The rest of the civilized world deplored the persecution of the Jews, but kept their doors locked.

What makes the Shanghai story unique is the flowering of life that developed despite the hardships and deprivations the Japanese imposed both on the Chinese and the Jews who fled Nazi persecution. Fortunately, the Japanese did not accede to the German demands to "solve the Jewish problem." They did not kill us.

A microcosm of central European Jewish life managed to

establish itself in this alien environment. We were the only trans-planted community to survive the war intact.

This is the story of siblings, a brother and a sister uprooted from their home and transported to a new life. Deborah was only three years old and Ilie twelve when this journey began. It is the story of escape and survival as seen through the eyes of two children and their different memories of the period that shaped their lives.

This is our story.

Deborah Strobin and Ilie Wacs

P_{ART} I

VIENNA

BROTHER

It is said that on the day of my birth, there arose a great argument
between my Romanian Papa and the Austrian rabbi. When Papa
announced my name would be Ilie, spelled with an "I" and not the
traditional "E," the rabbi put up a fight. He protested vehemently.
"You cannot use this name! What kind of name is that?" Ilie with
an "I" is the Romanian spelling of the name found only within the
Romanian borders. If it weren't for a Romanian tennis ace, whose
first name was Ilie and who dominated the game in the 1970s, I
would have gone to my grave questioning the veracity of the spelling
of my name. The Austrian rabbi, of course, could not care less about
Romanian spelling. This is Austria! He knew only what he knew on
that day, December 11, 1927, and what he knew for certain was that
Ilie was spelled with an "E" not an "I."

Papa was a stubborn man, a proud man, and to make matters worse, an atheist. Rabbis were to be tolerated only for the sake of his observant wife. He certainly didn't need one's permission to name his firstborn son. Papa yelled at the rabbi. He yelled at everyone. He yelled, "If I want to call him Cheng Chi, I can do that." The argument continued between the two men, focusing its reasoning on the Jewish name Eliahu, the name of a famous rabbi, and its permutations. Papa may not have been religious, but he was well read and a linguistic purist. Mutti, our mother, white knuckled, became quite anxious. She hated when Papa got upset. She always worried about his blood pressure. Finally, the rabbi threw up his hands and relented. Had he pressed much harder, Mutti was convinced her son would have wound up with the name Cheng Chi, but the rabbi had met his equal in Papa. Ilie it would be. He almost predicted it, Papa, right then and there on the day of my birth. He almost predicted we would be Chinese.

SISTER

My brother, Ilie, is the only member of our family who has been known through the entirety of his life solely by his birth name. Maybe this is because Papa fought so hard for the right to name his child. Maybe it's because the spelling was so unusual that there were no cute reductions. No nicknames to be found. Or maybe it's because Ilie was the golden son, the only son and the favored child, the firstborn and the gifted. Maybe his name came to signify the importance of his existence. Ilie. There is only one.

The same did not hold true for me. My name like my life seemed to be dependent entirely upon the whims of those who surrounded me. My first name was Dorit, D-O-R-I-T, which was either my grandmother's real name or her nickname. Either way, it's the name that was given to me in the Viennese hospital where I was born.

Mutti had no problems during her pregnancy or her labor with me. If she'd had problems, I would have heard about it. In those days, if a mother had a tough time giving birth, she let the kid know so they'd feel indebted forever. Mutti never complained so she must have had an easy time.

Papa hadn't wanted another child. He had Ilie, who was nine years older than me. I was unexpected. This isn't something a child should know about itself, but it's something Mutti blurted out during one of our arguments. Mutti was not a mother who pulled me aside for girl talk. Information was passed confrontationally.

Initially, Ilie hadn't been happy about my arrival, either. He was used to being the center of my parent's universe. He couldn't understand why the family needed another person, particularly a redheaded baby girl who demanded a lot of attention. He suggested that they send me back, and when that didn't work, he asked the nanny to take me home with her.

So I grew up with the name Dorit and knowing I was unwanted even if as I grew older, I could tell my parents cared about me. They were protective. I was waited for by a watched window. They never encouraged me to go out at night and not come back home. In some respect, this alleviated my fears even though I knew Papa was disappointed with the mere existence of a second child, a daughter. His disappointment turned me into a people pleaser. It crippled me with a shyness that most people interpreted as arrogance. It was a haunting.

Still, I adored Papa. My brother and me, we both did. We called our parents, Mutti, German for mother, and Papa. Mutti's real name was Helen though Papa called her Henya. Close enough. Mutti never called Papa by his first name, which was Maurice. She always called him by his last name, Wacs. "Oh, hi Wacs," she'd say as he walked in the door. They were no Ozzie and Harriet, our parents. For most of our childhood, Ilie and I never knew our father had a first name. Maybe calling my father by his first name would have been too endearing for Mutti. Too intimate.

So Wacs he was, at least to Mutti. To the Germans and the Austrians and the Chinese and the Americans and the Canadians, he would be known as Maurice, then Morris, and then Moritz, in no particular order just like Mutti would become Helen, Helah, Henia, or Henya. Ilie and I would not be allowed to take our father's last name, and we would instead carry the last name of Fach, Mutti's maiden name, until we made it to China where I would be dubbed Doris instead of Dorit then Debbie then finally, on my naturalization papers and on an old birth certificate, I would find my birth name, Deborah, which I had never, ever once been called in my entire life.

I took that name and used it as my own. Deborah. Deh-BORE-ah. Finally, I knew who I was even if everyone still called me Debra.

BROTHER

Papa was born Moritz Wacs, one of nine children, most of them sons, most of them tailors, all of them brought up Orthodox. His father, Mendel Wacs, was in the wine business in Romania, not the making of it, the selling of it. When he was sixteen years old, Papa was drafted into the Romanian army to fight in the First World War against the Austro-Hungarian Empire as part of the British and French alliance. The Romanian army was largely anti-Semitic, so the Jewish soldiers did not fight so avidly for their cause. There were Jews on both sides of the front, Romanian and Polish, who would not lift a gun against each other. They did not care about the war. Being Jewish in Poland or being Jewish in Romania, it was the same life. All Jews were persecuted. They might have been wearing different uniforms, but underneath they were the same. Why in the world would they fight each other?

Papa was one of these drafted reluctant boys. He'd been stationed at the Polish border where Jews were crossing back and forth at will. It was during one of these crossings that Papa abandoned his post. There was no way he could have known, as a sixteen-year-old boy with a gun in his hands, that his decision to cross the border and never return to Romania would affect every single second of his future, that it would determine the fate of every member of his future family. So he crossed.

He was declared a deserter and taken as a prisoner of war by the Austrians. He was allowed to settle in Austria though he could not become a citizen without a release from the Romanian government, a release that had to be acquired in person. There was no way to return to Romania. He would have been shot on sight. Papa was declared stateless. His marriage to our mother was not recognized. His children could not carry his last name. Years had passed, but that single act of teenage defiance was stubbornly clinging to Papa's present day. His desertion turned out to be our family's blessing and its curse.

SISTER

Every child thinks their mother is beautiful, but Ilie and I had irrefutable proof that Mutti was truly gorgeous. The proof was not her striking, long, dark hair, her warm smile, or her piercing green eyes, the kind of green you can see from a distance. The proof was not that she resembled Ingrid Bergman or that men of all ages, young and old, took notice of her everywhere we went. No, the proof that our mother was stunning was that she had literally been stopped on the streets of Vienna, asked to enter a beauty contest, and had walked away with the crown and a sash that read "Miss Vienna." Just like that.

Her reign as Miss Vienna was brief and fruitless. Shortly after winning, she was introduced by her sister to a Romanian ex-soldier much to the dismay of her deeply religious family. She was the daughter of Jacob and Deborah Fach. Her dad was in the soda business. He made seltzer water. They were well off. Romanians had a bad reputation, and to further their discontent, Moritz Wacs was stateless, a deserter, and no longer interested in honoring his Orthodox roots. Mutti's family just about threw themselves out their windows when she decided to marry him.

Papa was a very jealous man. Possessive. He didn't want anyone else admiring Mutti. When they attended dances or events, she danced only with him, and he certainly would not stand for her prancing about on a stage to run for Miss Austria. Her beauty-queen days were over, and so were her working days. Mutti had been a millinery designer, but Papa was a proud man, a provider, "You don't work. I work." Mutti became a housewife and a mother though her time as a designer heavily influenced her own personal fashion sense. She wore furs and custom suits, stylish hats and upswept hairdos. She was, as we say, a looker.

Ilie says my parents were happy in Vienna, and I have to believe him. But the vast majority of my personal memories of Mutti center on her attempts to keep a calm home in the midst of Papa's chaotic storm. She worried incessantly. She did everything in her power to keep Papa happy. She was convinced his blood pressure would kill him. She was constantly shushing and soothing and attempting to stabilize his moods. She was a woman who never made waves. No matter how bad things got, she adhered to a policy of stoicism. "If you cry, Dorit, you cry alone. Nobody wants to be your friend if you cry. Nobody wants to be with you if you're unhappy."

I feared my parents because they were my elders. The older generation was the enemy you lived among. I longed for affection from them both, but they were strangers to me and to each other. They behaved as if they were siblings. If they were in love, it didn't show, though in our home, love was not dinnertime conversation. For that matter, problems weren't either. Everybody had problems. They didn't make you special. It was better to just eat and keep quiet. So Ilie and me, we kept quiet and tried to understand as our parents conversed in one of the six or seven languages they shared in common. They spoke in German until they realized we understood their secrets. They switched to Yiddish, and when it was clear we'd picked that up, too, they switched to Russian with a smattering of Polish, Romanian, or Italian.

It did not matter that the languages themselves were romantic. I still couldn't tell if my parents were in love, so I became quite possessive of Mutti, almost jealous of the time she spent with Papa. When my parents having finally made it to New York ordered a double bed for our apartment, I demanded that they return it and order two twin-size beds as a replacement. I wanted to protect Mutti. I did not want to share her with anyone, Papa included.

Mutti was my everything. I idolized her. Mutti shone so brightly, I felt invisible. Men fawned over her. They tipped their hats and smiled, but Mutti held great respect for my father. She was loyal in the face of limitless advances. She had opportunities galore. She never took them. Her undeniable beauty confirmed my deepest fear about myself . . . that I was ugly. I knew I was ugly because I had red hair like Ilie. The redhead genes glided over my Papa's bald head and totally ignored Mutti, but as they had done to most of our aunts and uncles, they burdened me with a full head of bright, red, frizzy curls. I had hair that could not be tamed. Hair that required bows and brushing and energy to manage. Hair that instantly turned Ilie and me into outsiders among outsiders. Two redheaded stateless Jewish kids in Hitler's Austria, then again in the Japanese occupied Shanghai. We were pointed at, made fun of, the Japanese called us "red devils." Invisibility was the better option. I took it. I learned to keep my mouth shut and to blend into walls. I was a ghost.

BROTHER

There were probably two hundred thousand Jews in Vienna. We accounted for only 10 percent of the population in a primarily

Catholic country. Despite our being the minority, there was a very active Jewish community. We celebrated the high holidays with an enormous amount of eating and going to temple—without Papa, of course. Papa was totally irreligious; a free thinker, a leftist who knew Trotsky. At eighteen, he'd been politically active. He'd been involved in the Communist uprising in Hungary, and to me, it seemed as if there were mysterious comings and goings throughout our home. Papa was raised Orthodox, but he hated it. He hated rabbis and he wouldn't set foot in a temple. He kept a kosher home out of deference to Mutti, but you'd never find him in a pew, wearing a yarmulke to honor the season. I didn't last much longer in those pews myself. Most of the time, I snuck outside to play. Still, I knew those were days of great importance. There was a spirit of festivity in the air. It mattered to Mutti, and that meant it mattered to me.

Despite the closeness of our community, Vienna was a tough place to grow up Jewish. Even before the Nazis marched in, prejudice was part of my daily life. I attended a Catholic primary school with only five other Jewish boys in my class. I hated school. Every morning, we were made to step outside the classroom while the teacher led our classmates in prayer. He felt our being Jewish was a disruption. I had no non-Jewish friends my own age. Even among seven-year-olds, there was open hostility. That bred our reactionary, defensive hostility, and that antagonistic dynamic became cyclical. There was no camaraderie to alleviate the tension.

After school, I was chased home by the biggest boys. Fortunately, I was a fast runner. On the days I couldn't run fast enough, I was bullied or beaten. I always fought back. Sometimes, I won.

The only thing redeeming about Vienna was the chocolate. For breakfast, I drank hot chocolate with a Semmel, a substantial, chewy roll with a delicately crispy crust. For my post lunch snack, I had a chocolate sandwich, a Kaiser roll with a bar of chocolate stuffed inside. Chocolate for breakfast and chocolate after lunch. Healthy eating was not part of our upbringing. Everything was salty and greasy and fat. I hated fat. I hated boiled chicken. Most of what I was fed, I'd pretend to eat and then spit it out as soon as I could get to a bathroom. I was a lousy eater and a loud complainer.

I begged my parents, "Why don't we leave Vienna? Can't we go to America?" I was radical at the age of seven. My parents thought a change in schools might help. They attempted to enroll me in the arts school. At three years of age, Mutti found me sitting at the kitchen table, pencil in hand, drawing choo-choo trains. They were perfectly recognizable trains with wheels and a caboose and smoke pouring out of the chimney. I learned to occupy myself with drawing or fashioning paper into airplanes. After work, Papa brought home little toys. I would reach into the pocket of his suit jacket and gleefully grab his gift, which I promptly took apart. I had to see what made it tick, what made it go. I never managed to put them back together. Papa swore he'd never buy me anything else, but every evening, there would be a tiny, new toy. It was very clear to my parents that I was meant to be an artist. They enrolled me in the Art School, and at first, I was accepted, but then the offer was rescinded. I was Jewish. I wasn't allowed to attend. My parents did not sugarcoat my rejection. They told me flat out why I couldn't go. I was a Jew.

My parents were angry about anti-Semitism, not fearful. They fostered an attitude of superiority as protection, "They don't want to talk to us. Well, who wants to talk to them?" Papa wanted no part of trying to win people over. Mutti stayed close to home and kept us at her ankles. This was their way of coping, but it was not the method employed by all the Austrian Jews. There were Austrian Jews who considered themselves German. They couldn't understand why they were being persecuted. They converted to Catholicism in order to assimilate. They thought this would protect them.

The Eastern European Jews were tougher. My parents held less of an illusion about the true nature of Germany, the culture. Persecution was expected. It was a fact of life. There weren't pogroms like those in Russia, but there was certainly a policy of discrimination and in my case, on that run home from school every day, intimidation. There was just enough freedom extended to keep us from feeling threatened. We should have felt more threatened. Maybe then we would have seen it coming.

With arts school no longer an option and Papa's business doing well, we moved elsewhere in the second district, which was referred to as the Jewish district. Papa found us an apartment closer to the edge of the first district where those that thought more highly of themselves lived. It was the "good part" of Vienna, a large apartment overlooking the Dianabad, the extravagant and mammoth, famous stone building that loomed above the Donaukanal with its six floors of baths and a huge indoor swimming pool where my older cousin played water polo for the Vienna Hakoah, a Jewish sports club.

Our previous apartment had been situated over the headquarters of the Social Democratic Party, which was a hotbed of political activity. Meetings were held there every day. The men wore uniforms with armbands brandishing three black arrows in a circle and hats with feathers in the bands. I liked to draw those men in their uniforms. I copied the logo from their armbands, the circle with the three arrows, until Mutti got upset and tore up my drawings. She whispered, "Those meetings are illegal. It won't be so smart to have an apartment filled with these arrows!" I didn't understand. I was just drawing what I saw every day like other kids draw trees or birds flying.

As young as I was, I still could sense a growing discontent. There began to be long political discussions around the dinner table. My parents' friends came and went, bringing news. Conversations in our home were at full volume, always. As a kid, I was put to bed and not allowed to listen, but when your parents and their friends are screaming around the dinner table, you pick up things. I listened as they yelled about Chancellor Engelbert Dollfuss, who'd been in power since 1932. He had police bar entrance to the National

Council (Austria's lower house of parliament), effectively eliminating democracy in Austria. He declared himself dictator by emergency decree and gave himself absolute power.

Dollfuss didn't like the new chancellor of Germany, a man named Adolf Hitler, and he was worried that the Socialists and Communists might be gaining popularity. He banned and arrested members from all other Austrian parties including the Social Democrats, those men I had drawn with their armbands and feathered hats. His action spurred a miniature civil war in East Austria. The resistance was suppressed by police and military power, and the Social Democrats were outlawed. Its leaders were imprisoned or fled.

Five months later, Dollfuss was assassinated by ten Austrian Nazis in an attempted coup d'état called the July Putsch. Mussolini mobilized the Italian army on the Austrian border and threatened Hitler with war should he invade Austria to thwart the putsch. The Nazi assassins in Vienna surrendered and were executed, and Kurt Schuschnigg became the new chancellor of Austria.

In other words, command of the Austrian government was tenuous at best. Times were tenuous, and everyone was nervous. Living atop the outlawed Socialists was, perhaps, not the safest place to raise a family. So we moved to the edge of the first district into a larger apartment with a second-floor terrace and a beautiful ceramic-tiled radiator that stretched from floor to ceiling and kept us all warm. Papa's business moved with us. Papa had been working as a tailor for a big firm. Each tailor was responsible for three or four suits a week. Papa was so fast he could fill that order in two days and take the rest of the week off. His efficiency was resented, so he left and opened his own business as a custom tailor and men's designer.

His tailors and customers took over not only one large room in our apartment, but the entirety of our existence. Papa became the prima donna, the Picasso of tailors, and the sun around which we orbited. He stood all of five feet six inches tall from the top of his bald head to the bottom of his dandy spats, but that didn't stop him from strutting like a peacock, leading with his tummy, roly-poly. His reputation, like that tummy, preceded him and allowed him the freedom to tolerate no fools. If a man came to buy a suit, Papa would pull out a catalog and announce, "This is what you should have!" Design was in his genes. He had an eye for proportion, a great sense of style, and he knew instinctively how long and wide a lapel should be. These are things you can't teach. He'd choose the fabric and the color, and that constituted the whole of the discussion about the matter. Customers were to remain quiet, or they would be thrown out. During the fittings, they were not allowed to say one word, but his customers were always happy with the end result, so they came back. They also referred their friends, and Papa's business grew.

We settled into a comfortable, upper-middle-class life. I enrolled in a new school with Catholic teachers and an entirely Jewish student body. I was able to walk home instead of running, and Papa's tailors served as excellent soccer buddies, particularly Alois, a key tailor in the business. Alois was significantly younger than Papa, but he'd worked for him for a long time. Blonde, skinny, tall, and balding, for as long as I could remember, Alois had been around. He was more than a fixture. He was family.

On the days when Papa would get aggravated with me for playing soccer with Alois inside the apartment, I'd be thrown out, exiled to the terrace, and told to stay. I'd spend my time, carefully folding sheets of paper into airplanes. I'd send them gliding through the air, watch them ride what little currents they could catch, wafting and circling toward the Dianabad. I'd lean over the railing to see them fall to the ground below. There were good moments in Vienna. Contented, quiet moments in that apartment. Life in Vienna got a little bit better before it got a whole lot worse.

SISTER

I remember only snippets of my childhood in Vienna. Images that appear like a dream, stories overheard and incorporated as if they are memories, photos that substitute as experiences. I was a toddler when we fled, maybe three years old, much too young to make sense out of the sensory. So now I live with these fragments that reveal themselves at times so boldly I can feel them. This is why I believe they are true.

I see the apartment where we lived. There was a terrace or a veranda that wrapped around the back. There were two big double doors, French doors that opened from our living room. I looked out over green. Maybe a park. I was put to bed in a brown, wooden crib. People would stand by my crib, peer over, and look down on me. They liked to watch me balance little balls on my toes. It made them laugh. It made me laugh, too. Papa would sing and hum. Only later would I recognize that he hummed Puccini's operas and the one about the clown and *Carmen*. Most vividly, I see the Ferris wheel, the centerpiece of the Prater amusement park inside Vienna's Second District. It is overwhelming, a panorama wheel, like the front tire of a giant's bicycle, lit up and dangling carriages of crying kids, protective parents. I felt so tiny, standing in its glow, looking up and up and up to see where the people went to touch the clouds. It is a true memory for me. Just a sliver of my Viennese childhood that I can call my own.

The rest of my memories are false, generated by black-and-white photos of Papa and Ilie, dressed in suits and hats, facing the camera with broad smiles. I hadn't even been born yet, but the photos are incorporated into the fabric of me. I have a memory of Ilie laughing on the train ride that circled the park. I know that he never got enough of that train, but that memory and that knowledge are misplaced hand-me-downs. They live within me like squatters taking up residence in an abandoned building. Uninvited, restless, and secretive.

On occasion as I'm drifting off to sleep, I'll have the kinesthetic feeling of being lifted and saved. It was there at the Prater that Mutti took me on a canal ride. We were in a gondola, Mutti holding me in her arms. The tunnel was dark with strange figures hiding in the shadows, meant to frighten. Something scared me, popped out at me, and I was jolted. I tried to run away. I fell out of the gondola. The water was cold. I wasn't afraid to drown. Somebody dragged me back into the boat.

That's the most vivid memory. Of having something come at me. Of being scared and trying to run away. Of hitting the cold water. Of not being afraid to drown. Of having gotten away and then that feeling of being lifted up and out of the water. "Rescued."

I hate that feeling.

I hate it.

Somebody is always dragging me back into that damn boat.

BROTHER

Our new chancellor Schuschnigg called for a plebiscite on the independence of Austria. There would be a vote as to whether Austria should join Nazi Germany or not. All over Vienna were hung signs that read "SCHUSCHNIGG JA!" meaning "Schuschnigg Yes!" support the new chancellor or "NEIN," a big simple "No" in bright, bold letters encouraging Austrians to vote against an alliance with Germany. It seemed certain Schuschnigg would get his wish, but Hitler was not going to stand by as Austria declared its independence by public vote. Hitler issued an ultimatum: Hand over Austria, or face an invasion.

Overnight, the posters were ripped down and replaced with those reading "ANSCHLUSS JA!" encouraging the "union" of Austria with Germany. Windows were draped with swastika flags, and the same Austrians who voted "nein" the night before now lined the avenues, enthusiastically tossing flowers and waving flags. They hailed Hitler as a liberator. They cheered him wildly. They welcomed him with open arms. It was called the Blumenkrieg, the war of flowers. He was met with not one ounce of resistance. He was greeted with flowers.

Schuschnigg was arrested since he was one of the few Austrians to vocally oppose Hitler, ineffectively, but visibly. Mutti and Papa quickly got me off the sidewalks and safely into the apartment. We watched Hitler's welcoming parade from our second-floor windows. For hours and hours, we heard the clicking of those hobnail boots on the cobblestone streets. I wasn't afraid of the goose-stepping soldiers or intimidated by the saluting, the flags, and the steel helmets. I was very, very angry.

My new school closed for two days, and when it reopened, my favorite teacher appeared in class wearing a red armband with a black encircled swastika tied to his upper arm. He'd always been a friendly man, I liked him very much, but that morning he was remote and stern.

He announced, "From now on, everything is different. You are guests in this country, and you must conduct yourself accordingly."

All the boys just looked at each other. We were completely confused.

That day, I walked home with my friends. We asked each other, "What is he talking about?"

One boy asked me, "I was born here. How can I be a guest in the country where I was born?"

Even I, who was considered stateless because of Papa's war desertion, could not grasp the concept of being a visitor. All my life had been spent in Vienna. It was my home. More confusing was this directive to "conduct oneself accordingly." According to what?

I told my parents what happened. I was angry. "My teacher had the nerve to call us guests!"

Mutti became instantly fearful. She shushed me harshly. "Do not raise your voice. You're going to get us in deep trouble."

She was agitated in a way I didn't recognize. It frightened me. She threatened me. "Papa will end up in Dachau. Would you like that, Ilie?"

This threat of Dachau, it did not chill my heart the way it does now. Dachau was at that time a work camp, not a death camp. It could be avoided if you watched your step or if you were lucky enough to be stopped by a German soldier instead of an Austrian soldier. Everyone knew with a German soldier, you were much better off. You could talk your way out of trouble. He would let you go home. The Austrians were much more fervent, much less tolerant. They enjoyed watching Jews wash the pavements with toothbrushes; they smashed windows and were particularly cruel to older people or those who were visibly religious, wearing yarmulkes. Austrians dragged detainees straight to a police station, the gateway to Dachau, without so much as a skip in their step.

Our uncle, Bernhard, had been in Dachau. He'd failed to come home for lunch, and a call came from the police telling my aunt that he'd been taken into "schutzhaft," a euphemism for protective custody. Protective custody? Protected against whom? No one meant my uncle harm other than those claiming to be his "protectors," those who had beaten him on the streets while dragging him to Dachau. Our aunt was told to bring a change of clothes to the station. He would be gone for a while. Uncle Bernhard was released three weeks later looking, to my aunt's complete relief and bewilderment, healthy, tan, and fit. He'd been assigned to outdoor fieldwork, and he lost weight, gained muscle, got color. They made him shovel. He was a watchmaker who spent his life hunched over a table, futzing with tiny parts, always indoors. He never went outside. Three weeks in Dachau, he looked good. So the threat of Papa being thrown into Dachau for me mouthing off about my teacher held no weight with me. Papa was a roly-poly man. He was Jackie Gleason with a quick temper and high blood pressure. A few weeks in Dachau had done wonders for my uncle. Maybe Papa could use some exercise.

I was a stupid child. I didn't understand. None of us really understood. We weren't worried about the camps because we saw people walking in and out of them. We knew they had been detained for ridiculous reasons. We heard rumors about beatings and mistreatment. It was said that in Germany, detainees were beat with the butt of rifles, but those were the camps in Germany, not Austria. Friends and family who ended up in Dachau walked out alive and in the case of my uncle, healthier.

As a kid, the Nazis seemed less like a threat and more like a big inconvenience. I adapted Papa's bravado about the whole affair. He declared the Nazis impotent. "The British and French will never allow Hitler to get away with this. He's overreaching. They'll make mincemeat out of him." Papa read every newspaper. He had his ear to the ground. I believed him. I was buoyed by his confidence. Papa walked through the streets with a swagger in his step, the peacock tailor, his head held high because Papa had one thing most other Jews did not. Papa had a guardian angel: the protection of the Swiss government.

When Papa deserted the Romanian army and was taken as a prisoner of war, the Swiss general consulate in Budapest gave him a document that folded like an accordion. It was stamped with numerous seals, peppered with official signatures, and looked exceedingly official. The document basically said, "The Swiss General Consulate asks that the bearer of this document be given the full protection of and every courtesy is to be extended to him by the government where he resides at the moment."

This document was the great blessing of his desertion. Every time a German soldier said, "Papers, please," Papa would take out that accordion-folded talisman, present it, and then the soldier would salute him and let us go. The fact that the documents were dated 1917 meant nothing to them. All they saw were those seals and those stamps and those signatures. They felt my father was a man under protection. He was never arrested.

But his desertion was also our curse. Now that the Nazis were running Vienna, all Jews with foreign citizenship were being threatened with deportation. Papa was a stateless person with protective papers, but neither the Austrian nor the German government recognized his marriage. Mutti was Polish, so my sister and I were considered Polish citizens with Polish passports. Just because Dorit and I were born in Austria didn't make us Austrian citizens. We were Jews and Polish Jews at that. We would not be allowed to stay.

Except that we were. Papa's employee, the tailor Alois, had become an active member of the Nazi Party. A member yes, but what he heard at the rallies did not mesh with things as he saw it. Papa had always treated him well. I was his favorite soccer buddy. Alois knew for a fact that we did not have horns. He began to protect us. We became his Jews. As he rose through the ranks of the Nazi Party, he secured extensions for Mutti so we wouldn't have to leave Austria. The extensions came in six-month increments. Six months, six months, six months.

Mutti's mornings became an exercise in futility. We needed to leave Vienna. We had affidavits of support from our family in the United States promising that we would not be a burden on the American government should we be allowed to enter its borders, but the quotas for both Polish and Romanian refugees had long been met. The waiting lists were infinite as were the lines outside every consulate's office. A rumor would spread that Canada or Australia had opened its borders, and Mutti would run to stand in front of their consulate only to find that the rumor was just that, inaccurate hearsay. Empty continents would not let us in. Every country had restrictions, even the ones nobody could locate on a map. The family sponsoring you had to be a sibling or a first cousin, but not so many Jews had a brother in, say, the Philippines. Those lucky enough to receive visas were burdened with paying enormous taxes to both the Austrian and the German governments before departure and were required to leave all their possessions behind. Leaving was not an attractive option. Mutti kept trying regardless. She stood in line, the Jewish Miss Vienna, a far cry from walking the beauty-pageant stage of her reign. The woman who had only a few years earlier been hailed as the beautiful face of her city was no longer welcome there. She was to be thrown out, disowned, discarded, and us along with her.

Around this time in Paris, a young man named Herschel Grynszpan received a postcard from his sister. His family, along with twelve thousand other Polish Jews, were ripped from their homes in Germany, told to pack a single suitcase, and marched across the river to Poland with no food and no shelter in the pouring rain. The Polish refused their entry and sent them back to Germany. The Germans reciprocated by doing the same, and this went on for four days. Finally, Poland admitted a few thousand, but the rest were stuck, starving and destitute in a refugee camp at the border.

Grynszpan was distraught upon receiving his sister's postcard. He began to petition the German embassy in Paris, and when he was ignored, he chose to take matters into his own hands. He bought a revolver and a box of bullets. He arrived at the German embassy and asked to see an official. He was taken to the office of Ernst von Rath, a German diplomat, whom he shot three times. He made no attempt to escape. In his pocket, he carried a postcard that read, "I must protest so that the whole world hears . . ." Unfortunately, the Germans were the only ones listening.

Being a young boy, I didn't know what happened in Paris. I didn't know who vom Rath was or that because of his death, a man named Joseph Goebbels delivered a speech commanding Nazi Party leaders to organize a pogrom. I had no way of knowing that another man named Reinhard Heydrich, director of the Reich, was sending secret telegrams with specific instructions as to how the riots should be carried out, or that the police had been given orders to seize Jewish archives from synagogues and to arrest all "healthy male Jews, who are not too old" for immediate transfer to the concentration camps. All I knew was this: Alois came to our house. His tone was quite grave, and he convinced Papa that something terrible was going to happen. I could tell it was dangerous for him even to be seen in our home. He told Papa, "Gather your family tonight. Tell them to come here. Keep everyone inside. You will not be touched."

Mutti's sister was quickly summoned. She arrived with her husband, their daughter and son-in-law. Her two sons had already fled Vienna. There was no time to pack up their belongings. We stayed away from the windows with all the lights out and the curtains drawn. We kept very still and quiet. Then, we waited. It didn't take long before the silence filled with the shattering explosion of glass. The night wore on, a cacophony of sledgehammers and axes breaking down doors, women screaming, babies crying, men yelling at other men. There was the acrid smell of smoke, fires burning somewhere, not in our building, and the horrifying scuffle of people and furniture being dragged out of their homes and into the streets. We heard the chaos coming closer. Our building did not have an elevator, only stone steps. I stood inside the door, and I heard hobnail boots coming up, click, click, click, and click. I heard men's voices. I heard the boots stop at our door, and then I heard them move on. They never even knocked. We were passed over. We were shielded by Alois. We were saved.

At that moment, I could not feel grateful for our miraculous blessing. I could not even feel fear. All I could feel in my heart at that exact moment was a hateful, caustic, rage. I hated Vienna. I hated Austria. I hated the Germans. I hated my teacher with his stupid armband. I hated people I used to love. I hated that we were hated.

We stayed locked in our apartment for two days. We needed food and had to emerge to face the new world order that now existed outside our front door. The pogrom, Kristallnacht, had been particularly brutal. Most of the city's synagogues were burned to shells. All the Jewish-owned businesses were vandalized and ransacked. Thousands had been deported to Dachau and Buchenwald. There was glass everywhere. The city was devastated.

My parents could no longer shelter me from the reality. Though I was only eleven, I was no longer a little boy. My fearlessness, my security, my confidence in Papa's bravado, they were all gone. I held great fear for my parents. Whenever they left the house, I stood by the windows until they came home again. I understood now that the streets were not safe. I became hyperaware of people walking behind me. Still, to this day, if I hear footsteps behind me, I cross the street. Everything had changed. I knew it was possible for any one of us to be taken at any moment. I was terrified we would be abandoned. I lived in a constant state of apprehension. There was no babysitter there to comfort me. I sat for myself. My sister sat for herself. We sat together by the windows, and we waited, and even if I saw Papa on the sidewalk below, I would not relax until he was inside our home with the door locked.

The situation was now dire. Alois made that very clear. He secured one last extension for my mother, but told Papa in no uncertain terms to "get out of the country by August 31, 1939." A very specific date with great significance. The war broke out one day later, but we were already gone. Not because we were smarter or more strategic, but because we were lucky. Luckily, Papa had deserted and ended up with POW documentation. Luckily, he had hired a young man named Alois. Luckily, Alois had the strength, the courage, and the heart to endanger his own life to save ours. We had stayed in the country of Austria, the city of Vienna, and the state of denial for as long as we could. We had to go.

What became of Alois, I do not know. I don't know if he survived the war or who he turned out to be when he was later drafted into Hitler's army. All I know is he helped us in ways that can never be repaid. My family escaped, and I am alive because of his actions. I never sought him out. I prefer not to know what became of him. I needed and still need the mystery that allows me to remember him as one of the good guys.

SISTER

She lied to me, Mutti, though I cannot bring myself to call her a liar because I know now, in hindsight, that her lies, her omissions, her stories were acts of protection, convoluted ways of expressing her love.

Mutti told me that she and Papa planned a romantic vacation for two in Italy. She told me our nanny wasn't available to babysit, and therefore, she and Papa had been forced to take us, the kids with them on their luxury cruise, which turned out to be a fortuitous turn of events. While we were traveling, the war broke out, and we were not allowed to return to Austria. She told me that we got stuck in Italy with just the clothes on our backs and that the only place we could travel to was China. She told me we were lucky.

This lie, her first lie (because there would be others), was given to me as a gift. It was told to me because I began to believe we had magically materialized in China. I couldn't remember Vienna at all. I was so young when we left, barely three years old. Still, I could look around and know I wasn't Chinese, so I had questions. Lots of questions. I heard people saying they had come from Germany or Poland, and I didn't know what that meant, "to have come from" some different place.

I asked Mutti, "Why are we here?"

She answered, "We went on a big ship."

I still didn't understand. "But where was I born?"

She answered, "In Vienna, Austria."

She spoke about a lush land dotted with beautiful castles. She talked about the popularity of zultz, a pressed pork shoulder, thinly sliced and served with vinegar and onions. Because she kept a kosher home, Mutti made her version with beef bones. She spoke about Sacher torte, the dark chocolate, flourless cake with raspberry jelly on the inside and chocolate icing with whipped cream on top. She spoke about bronze statues on pedestals, fountains, and opera houses. She spoke about beauty and culture and cleanliness. I could not understand why we left such a magical world. "Why didn't we stay there?" I asked. Thus was born the "we went on vacation and got stuck in Italy" story.

I had no reason to question my mother's explanation. Based on her story, I determined that everyone else had been on vacation, as well. These people I heard speaking about being "thrown out of their countries," that did not apply to me. My parents and I, we had gone on vacation. Nobody had thrown us out of anywhere. We were just away on a seemingly, never-ending, horrible, smelly, crowded vacation.

So many years later, I found a photograph of me sitting on the deck of a ship, propped up by a life preserver. I asked my brother about it, and he told me the tale of our journey from Vienna to Shanghai, how everyone kept hoping we'd be allowed to dock some-where, anywhere but China, how fresh water ran low, and every day brought a new route. He used the word refugee. I was confused by his version of events. The boat we were on was a pleasure cruise. Honey-mooners booked passage on it after their weddings. How could we have been refugees if we'd simply taken a vacation and gotten stuck away from home?

Ilie handled me gently. Yes, the boat was a luxury cruise ship, and yes, technically, we'd booked passage for what would have been, at any other moment in history, a pleasure cruise to Shanghai from Italy. It was just that at that particular moment in history, this cruise ship was filled with Jews. Jews running for their lives.

I heard his version, and I knew it was true, but deep down within the core of me, Mutti's lie had taken hold and become my truth. At a party in the Hamptons with Ilie, someone asks the usual ques-tions, "What do you do?" or "Where are you from?" I let Ilie do the talking because these are his friends, and he's the one who doesn't mind dredging up the past. He captivates the crowd, as always, he mentions the boat.

I cut in, with a breezy, "It's too bad they didn't let us into Italy.

Our parents paid for that vacation." Her lie bubbles up and out of my mouth, escaping my lips before a single, censoring thought can enter my mind.

Ilie stares at me as if I am insane, and still, it takes me a moment to realize what I've said. Mutti's myth has become my own. Her lie has become my lie. I repeat it aloud because it's better than admitting that our homeland, the beautiful country with delicious desserts and romantic castles would not have us. It's better than being a refugee.

P*ART II*

SHANGHAI

BROTHER

From those who fled before us, we received word about Shanghai, and the word wasn't good. Postcards came back describing a hot, dreadful, crowded city. Those who had gone wished they'd never left. China was so different. They could not acclimate. Everyone in Vienna knew Shanghai was a port of last resort. If you could go anywhere else, you did. We had no other option. Our last six-month extension to remain in Vienna expired, and Alois pressured Papa to take his word seriously. We had to be out of Austria by the end of August. Shanghai it was.

But leaving required much more than just packing our bags. Mutti, doing all the legwork, patiently dealt with the Austrian bureaucracy, making sure all the documents were signed, counter-signed, stamped, and certified. The Nazis had a thing for stamps and seals with ferocious-looking eagles—lots of eagles.

.   Between Papa's love of history and my insatiable curiosity, we both wanted to learn more and more about our new home-to-be. We started reading and sharing information. Papa told me that after the First Opium War had ended in the early 1840s, Shanghai grew from a fishing village into a massive treaty port. A treaty port ensured the port remained open to international trade rather than being surrendered in its entirety. A bunch of other treaty ports were established that allowed foreign nations to visit, live, and trade on Chinese soil. Treaty ports were the start of the foreign concessions all over China.

By "foreign concessions," they meant territories that were governed and occupied by foreign powers, usually Westerners or the Japanese. Almost like a colony. Each foreign power administrated their own concession, although the United Kingdom and United States agreed to merge. The British settlement formed south of Suzhou creek in the Huangpu district, while the American settlement took up residence north of Suzhou creek in the Hongkou district. Together, they created the International Settlement. The French Concession settled south of them.

The concessions had extraterritoriality. They functioned as enclaves. They had their own police forces and their own separate laws. A criminal could commit a crime in one concession, walk a few blocks down the road, and escape to another. Needless to say, organized crime flourished. So did the "Shaghailanders" or the ex-pats. Foreign citizens were making money hand over fist.

The Chinese were not so lucky. For a long time, they were forbidden to live inside the concessions and were literally second-class citizens on their own soil. Eventually, in the interest of having easy access to cheap labor, the Chinese were allowed to move in, though it did not much improve their lot. There was a Chinese mayor who'd been tasked with creating a new city center to include a public museum, library, sports stadium, and city hall. But he only lasted ten years. By the time we headed to Shanghai, the Japanese occupied the municipality, making Shanghai the only city in the world that did not require a visa, passport, or any other official documentation to enter. No government was truly "in charge" of Shanghai. There was no quota system in place. All you had to do was book passage and get on a boat.

That is, to be fair, a simplification of what it took to get to Shanghai. In truth, to book passage, my parents had to pay with American dollars. Austrian money had been completely devalued. It was essentially worthless, but the Germans would not allow Jews to have American currency. It was grounds for imprisonment. Damned if you did, damned if you didn't. Papa's family in Romania was contacted to see if they could help. The Romanian government was corrupt, and Papa's family lived in the mountains. They were rural people, far removed from any conflict. Papa couldn't go back to his hometown, but he was still in touch with his parents. They managed to secure American money, paid for our passage on an Italian luxury liner called the SS Conte Biancamano, and sent word that we should leave immediately. It was a good lesson in survival. If you're ever in a position where your life is in danger, get to a country with a corrupt government. There, you have a chance. There's always a door open, always a way to make a deal. Someone can be bribed.

Mutti's sister and her family drove us to the train station to say our goodbyes. They refused to leave with us. Even after a night like Kristallnacht and Uncle Bernhard's arrest, my aunt felt the war and its accompanying fanaticism would blow over. "Why leave just to come back again? Nothing's going to happen." Her attitude was the attitude of most. There was no mass exodus at the train station. There were no throngs of people. It was a train trip like any other train trip. There was no sense of impending disaster. There should have been. More people would have left. More people would have been saved. The only reason we were on that train was Alois' urgent and insistent demand that we go. Looking back, it's amazing that Papa in his stubbornness listened to him.

I knew the moment I got on that train I would never live in
Vienna again. I was super excited. I'd spent the whole of my young
life, all twelve years, desperately wanting to leave, and now, we were
finally on our way. I could tell my parents were upset, but in my
heart of hearts, I felt I was headed for a great adventure. A train
trip, a boat, the open sea. Italy, China. For a boy nearing thirteen,
this was a grand excitement. I would be on a boat heading into foreign waters. I hadn't a care in the world until our train stopped on
the Austrian-German side of the border for several hours. Officers
walked through each car asking for papers. Everyone on the train
became apprehensive. Anything could happen. It seemed an inter-
minable wait, but they finally made it to our car. Our papers were in
order, and we were allowed to cross. A great burden must have lifted
off of Mutti's shoulders at that moment. For nearly two years, on
nearly a daily basis, she had tried to secure a visa of any kind. There
would be no more waiting in line for Mutti. We were still stateless,
but we were free.

As we crossed the border from Austria into Italy, a brief pang of
upset caused my stomach to wrench. I heard nothing but Italian
being spoken, and the strangeness of that language worried me. The
reality of what was happening smacked my gut. We were leaving.
We would not understand what was being said. We would not be
in familiar territory. Everything would be strange, unknown, confusing. My panic lasted for exactly a second and a half. Then, I was
joyous.

No more bullies!

No more showing papers!

No more hiding in our apartment!

The train traveled overnight through the Alps, and we stayed for
two days in Milan. From there, we traveled to Genoa where I saw the
biggest boat I'd ever seen, the SS Conte Biancamano, a luxury liner
of the grandest sort. She was long, very straight with two gigantic
steam chimneys in her middle and three or four decks to house the

thousands of people she carried. Because we'd purchased our tickets so last minute, all of our possessions were loaded onto a German freighter to follow, and we weren't able to purchase a cabin large enough to accommodate our entire family. Papa and I were separated from Mutti and my sister to sleep, but we met for delicious communal meals and spent the days playing on the deck. At night, we retreated to our respective cabins with the bunk beds, little bathrooms, and portholes.

We were the last boat out.

The boat was overflowing with children from all over Europe: Germany, Austria and Poland ... I made friends with brothers from Berlin, Ingolf and Alfred. The Berliners spoke a different German than we did. I made fun of their German, and they made fun of mine. The food was good, my bunk bed was comfy, I got to run around all day and play with new friends. I loved the SS Conte Biancamano. It was a holiday that floated! I could have stayed on that boat forever.

At one point, that seemed a real possibility. The voyage was supposed to sail east through the Suez Canal through India and last five weeks. Then, the war reached us in the Suez Canal. The captain, sailing an Italian boat in Allied waters, feared the British would seize his ship. Fortunately, he could not turn around. He was surrounded by British waters. The next port of call was Calcutta, also British, so he struck south to the Indian Ocean. The crew posted maps, and each day, a sailor would stick a red pin into the map indicating our new position. All the kids would jostle each other to gather around the map. Ingolf and I wagered and wondered, "Where are we going today?"

We hoped we would end up in Australia. No such luck. We sailed through the Dutch East Indies, which was then called Sumatra and was neutral at that point. The Germans hadn't invaded the Dutch yet. It took us ten days to get there, three days longer than anticipated, so drinking water became scarce. It being an Italian ship, there was plenty of wine. We finally got to Batavia, which is now Jakarta, and they would not let us in. The captain had no choice but to take us to Shanghai. We sailed to Singapore, Manila, Hong Kong, and then Shanghai. I was a redheaded, twelve-year-old Jewish boy from Austria, and suddenly, I lived in China.

Coming off the boat, the first thing I saw was what appeared to be eighty million Chinese people converging on me personally! I had never seen so many people in my life. There were people everywhere! Men with rickshaws, men carrying things, men dragging things, kids running, women walking, everyone yelling and moving, and the noise, the noise, the noise! It was so loud and busy and frenetic, I didn't know where to look first. And the heat! It was oppressively hot. A constant blast of hot air and humidity. Combined with the seemingly millions of people, the hustle and the noise, I was completely overwhelmed. I did my best to stay with my parents and follow the crowd.

Despite the delays in our journey, our arrival was expected, and the boat was met by representatives from the Jewish relief organization there to help get us settled. The organization in charge at that time was the International Committee for European Immigrants, which most people called the I.C. or the Komor Committee. They were funded by an extremely wealthy man named Sir Victor Sassoon when it became clear that a massive effort was going to be needed. At first, the refugees had arrived by handfuls. They were housed in private homes and treated like visiting relatives. The early émigrés were far more financially secure than we were. They had time to organize their departure. They'd been allowed to keep their money and their personal possessions at the German border. They were better prepared to survive the move.

Then the numbers grew and grew and grew. Refugees began arriving by the hundreds and then the thousands. People needed housing, meals, jobs, and money. Sir Sassoon stepped up. He was an Iraqi Jew with British citizenship who owned most of Shanghai's real estate. He was the Rockefeller of Shanghai with wealth unimaginable. The man he hired to run the I.C. on his behalf was a Hungarian business-man named Paul Komor. They operated out of the Hotel Cathay, and we learned quickly that the refugees referred to them simply as the Baghdadi Jews.

The I.C. was well organized. They knew when ships were due and how many people to expect. They had the manifests. They prepped the beds, and once our boat emptied, they put us into open, flatbed trucks and drove us to an area called Hongkou. The truck bounced and swerved down the long streets. All I could see were signs that read "Post No Bills" in English. I thought Post No Bills must have been the name of the street. The trucks dropped us off at the one of the refugee dormitories, which were called Heim.

A Heim was essentially an armory of steel bunk beds with partitions made of sheets strung on ropes to separate families and also the men from the women. Food was provided, as were nurses and doctors. By the time we arrived in Shanghai, the Heim was being run by the refugees themselves. They'd taken over as more German speakers arrived since the locals spoke only Russian, English, and perhaps some Yiddish. The Heim held a few hundred people in one large room. It was filled with mostly the old, the ill, and those that couldn't take care of themselves. It was a jarring introduction to life in Shanghai, having just come off a luxury cruise liner with our own room and bathroom, tiny as they were, to find ourselves being herded like cattle into the overcrowded, hot human warehouse. We lasted one night at Heim. The next morning, Papa yelled, "Out! We don't live in a place like this!"

He began his search for our apartment among the mish-mosh of foreign concessions, a patchwork quilt divided by wars and their subsequent treaties. The French Concession was well out of our price range, occupied by the wealthier British and American merchants who built large homes among the Russian émigrés who'd fled during the revolution. To the east of them was the walled Chinese city and to the north was what remained of the International Settlement, which shared British and American concession that had flourished until the Japanese decided they wanted what the Chinese, British, and Americans had. By the time we moved to an apartment on Chusan Road in the center of the Hongkou District, it was the poorest section of Shanghai. The Americans and British were long gone, and the area was now occupied by the Japanese.

Our apartment was small, one room with an anteroom on the front that Papa used for his business. The larger of the two rooms functioned as our kitchen, our living space, and the bedroom to us all. The beautiful, floor-to-ceiling ceramic-tile radiator I so loved from our apartment in Vienna was replaced by a converted flowerpot that Mutti purchased and transformed into a hibachi with a grill top. That flowerpot acted as both our stove and our only source of heat. Our toilet was an outhouse at the back of the hall called the honey pot. Each morning, the boy who slept in the backyard and swept the halls would take the honey pot downstairs to the front of the building where a man would come by with a big cart. The boy would empty the pot, rinse it out a bit, and then return it to the outhouse. Conditions were primitive at best, but having spent one night at Heim, I knew we were better off on Chusan Road. Plus, the apartment was only temporary. China was only temporary. A way station of sorts. The limbo before the Promised Land. Our final destination was America.

If we'd had suitcases, we wouldn't have even bothered to unpack them.

SISTER

When I was seven, Papa made the curtain. It was gathered on top and hung straight down in front of the only closet we had. I used the closet when I wanted privacy to change my clothes, to bathe in the washbasin, or just to disappear from the world for a bit to think my own thoughts. It was my own personal hide-and-seek. I carved notches on the inside of the closet, counting my days like a prisoner. The days I served in Shanghai.

Tucked away in the closet, I grew to love the curtain. I liked to sit on the floor and count the flowers in the pattern. If there was a thread loose, I'd find it. Once I pulled at the delicate lining that had worn so thin, it tore without effort. I made three more tears and then braided the lining in such a way that only I would know how to find it again. It was my secret.

The curtain was like having a toy, which my parents couldn't afford. I only had one doll I named Susie, but she didn't have any arms. She was made of molded plastic, even her hair, and her eyes never closed. I wasn't attached to her the way some kids develop an obsession for their blanket. Papa even went so far as to make her new clothes, but she wasn't much of a friend to me. She was just a doll someone had thrown out and Papa found. There was nothing magical about her.

The curtain, however, was magical. I'd seen enough movies to know that when a curtain opened, a grand expanse should be revealed. I fantasized that one day, I would open my flowered curtain, and there would be a lovely, welcoming pool. I would open the curtain and see Shangri-la. I would open the curtain and be transported to the United States. I tried opening it dramatically. I tried sneaking a peek from behind it. Neither method worked. Every time I opened my curtain, all I saw was the same old table and chairs I lived with, the ones by my cot and Ilie's mattress on the floor.

My parents got me a cot because I was terrified to sleep on the floor with all the bugs. I'd been badly bitten by them, whereas Ilie was never bothered by them. He just shoved them away and went back to sleep. I couldn't. There were ants all over and holes in the walls that functioned as tunnels for roaches, rats, and mice. At night, I heard them squeaking. It made me extremely squeamish, a personality trait that has followed me through the rest of my life. Even still, I pretend to fluff the sheets before I get into any bed. In reality, I'm checking for bugs. Bugs bothered me more than being hungry. Bugs bothered me more than the filth.

It was the filth that drove Mutti crazy. She could not stand the conditions in which we lived. She wanted everything in her home to be pristine, which was impossible. The apartment building was old and falling apart. She spent her day hand washing our garments, ironing and mending. She would never allow me out the door with a spot on my dress, and if I soiled it while out, I was in big trouble. Cleanliness was demanded as strictly by Mutti as vaccinations were by the Japanese. The Japanese had shots for everything, and they made sure we got injections to ward off any possible disease. If one kid got sick in that densely populated city, the whole community would get sick. Without announcement, the Japanese would close off an entire city block and force everyone to show their inoculation papers. If you didn't have them with you, too bad, you got the shot whether you'd already had it or not. Poor Ilie came home needle-stuck over and over again, and those were big needles.

The vaccinations were just for the Jews. The Chinese, they treated like dirt. The Japanese hated the Chinese and could not have cared one iota less about them. The Chinese lived in miserable conditions, mostly crammed into the alleyways, numerous families in one room, while we were able to live along the more spacious streets. Chusan Road was, in fact, the main street of the Hongkou district. It functioned as a main center for commerce and activity, whereas the alleys were grimy, infested with lice, and a breeding ground for disease. I often passed kids being deloused by their parents. Mutti told me to stay clear, so I did.

Mutti's never-ending, losing battle against the filth was only made worse by the fact that we lived two doors down from the children's hospital. Every morning, there would be dead babies wrapped in newspapers or adult bodies wrapped in white sheets left outside its doors. Whoever had died the night before was left on our sidewalk. People couldn't afford to bury the dead. The dead were thrown out like garbage. It didn't scare me to see those bodies on the sidewalks. I quickly became desensitized to death. As young as I was, I learned that people died. Many people had died before me. A lot would die after. Dead bodies were like grass. Common. Mutti told me never to touch them, so I didn't. I jumped over the bodies on my way to school.

Mutti made me scrub and change clothes the minute I walked in the door. She would fill the basin with the tepid water and sprinkle a purple disinfectant powder into it. I wasn't allowed to use the communal bathroom on the second floor even though it had a shower and a bathtub. Everyone else in the family used the outhouse, but I had to sponge bathe myself in the washbasin. Even though Mutti never wanted me out of her sight, once I became a preteen, I insisted on bathing behind the curtain. The closet wasn't very wide or deep. There wasn't much space to move. Mutti would warn me, "Be careful you don't wet all our clothes hanging." I pushed the curtain forward to get more room.

It seemed to me I spent most of my childhood bathing or sleeping. Mutti put me down for a nap just about every two minutes. Ilie, too. Children were meant to be seen, but not heard. Naps got us out of the way in that cramped apartment, and if I was lucky, Mutti would let me nap in my parents' bed. It was bigger than my cot and had a metal headboard with slots. I loved how Mutti would rub my back in order to get me to sleep. It was a rare moment of affection from her, so desperately needed. I'd keep my eyes open just as long as I could so she would stay by my side. As I drifted off, I heard the Chinese men, on the street below our windows, selling their wares. I heard the coolie laborers running past, the Chinese men burdened with those heavy bundles hung from either end of a bamboo pole, carried across their backs and shoulders. They hummed a song, always the same song, less like singing and more like chanting a mantra. I did not know what they were chanting. I imagined it must have been about the heaviness of their load, the burdens of their lives. It was my daily lullaby.

At night, I wasn't allowed to sleep in my parents' bed. I had to sleep in my cot, but I didn't mind because nights were the highlight of my whole day. The sun would go down alleviating the oppressive heat, and everyone would gather on their stoops, their terraces, their stairs to relish the cooler air, spend some time together. Pretty much everyone in our building was Jewish, on all three floors, in all nine apartments. There were Chinese families living in the building that was attached, constructed as the mirror image of our building, but we didn't know those families. We stuck to our own.

Across the street was a whorehouse called the Little Barcelona Bar. I was either too young or too naive to understand its machinations. There were tables outside, in front of the bar, and women stood around, wearing short skirts with slits showing their legs. They dangled cigarettes from the corners of their mouths. Men were often face-down drunk on the tables. I thought they were taking naps. I thought the women rubbed their backs to help them fall asleep. Just like Mutti.

Watching the comings and goings of the Little Barcelona, I thought to myself, "That's a lot of aunts and uncles." I couldn't remember my extended family from Vienna. Mutti spoke about her sister, my aunt, but I had no image in my mind of her face. So anytime I saw an adult that resembled me in China, I wanted them to be my aunt or my uncle. I wanted a big family the way that Chinese families seemed to stick together, take care of their elderly, the young respecting the old. Chinese families were very close, maybe brought even closer by the Japanese occupation, the terrible conditions under which they lived. I saw them all the time, sitting on their stoops, circled around a hibachi, having their meals together, sharing what little they had to offer. Toddlers, babies, the grandparents, everyone had the meal together. There were moments when I forgot I was supposed to pity them, and instead, I wanted to change places.

I wished my family was as big as the families sitting in those circles. So in my head, everyone became "Auntie-this" or "Uncle-that," and sometimes, I'd slip and actually call an adult by my secret term of affection. They never cared. They never responded. I may as well have been saying, "Good morning."

I enjoyed those nights with my family and the neighbors on the stoop. Papa would buy me a Coca-Cola from the bar, and Mutti would gossip with the other mothers. Papa would sing an opera or teach us to how to tap dance. He was light on his feet, and as the sun faded, it seemed his humor rose, a companion to the moon. His temper would mellow, and he'd joke around, make us laugh and lighten our miserable situation. I'd do my best to imitate his dance moves. I'd tap one foot then the other foot and then heel-toe-heel-toe slow and then faster, heel-toe-heel-toe-heel. It made Papa smile, and for those few hours before bedtime, the fear would go away. I'd slowly sip my Coca-Cola, shuffle my tapping feet, and watch across the street as my surrogate aunts and uncles danced the night away.

BROTHER

First thing, each morning, it was my job to fill the hibachi flowerpot with charcoal and get the fire started by fanning the black coals with a bamboo fan. Once the coals were solidly red, Mutti would send me to buy boiling water. We had to be very careful about the water in our apartment and all over Shanghai. We could not drink the water from our tap. We couldn't eat any raw fruits or vegetables that hadn't been washed with sterile water. There were all kinds of horrible diseases running rampant: cholera, typhus, and dysentery were most prevalent. The Chinese used human waste as fertilizer, which is, in terms of quality and nutrients, the best, but extremely dangerous in terms of human health. Boiled water was essential, and our little hibachi couldn't keep us in adequate supply. The water had to be bought.

Mutti would give me the kettle or a thermos, depending on our needs, and I would go downstairs to the Chinese store that kept huge pots of water for sale. Water could be bought with sticks that were shaped like Popsicle sticks. That was the currency, and the sticks came in books of four or five. Once you offered your sticks, you had to wait for the water to come to a vigorous boil.

Very often, I got into an argument with the man who ran the store. He'd try to fill my kettle or thermos with water before it had boiled, but I wouldn't let him. I would insist, "Show me that it's boiling! Lift the lid! I want to see it!" He'd get quite angry with me, but sure enough, it wasn't boiling. I'd make him wait longer. "Now, it's boiling." He'd fill my thermos, and I'd march back home proud to have protected my family from sickness.

On the days I carried the thermos, Mutti made coffee, and I'd have coffee with condensed milk and a piece of bread with butter on it or maybe some jam. That would be breakfast. On rare occasions, Mutti would send me to buy water with a kettle filled with eggs. By the time I'd get back home, the eggs would be soft-boiled. Those were the luxurious days when we got to have a big breakfast. Ninety percent of the time, we ate polenta for breakfast, which Dorit hated. Food was not a constant. Eating was not taken for granted. If we had food, we ate what was put in front of us. I often went to school hungry.

I walked to school every morning with Bob, who later on would also be sponsored by Charlie Jordan, a hero who saved many lives. Bob's parents owned a Viennese restaurant, the Delikat, across the street from us. It was opposite the alley from the Little Barcelona Bar, and their customers were primarily the Russian and German Jews who fled earlier than the Austrians. In the '20s and '30s, almost twenty thousand so-called White Russians and Russian Jews fled the newly established Soviet Union and took up residence in Shanghai. They were the second-largest foreign community in the city, and they had a lot more money than us, so Bob's family restaurant was fairly successful. They ate well, at least consistently. I always envied

Bob his breakfast though I never told him I was hungry. It didn't seem like good walking conversation.

It wasn't a short walk to school. The building was in Hongkou, but not so close to our apartment. I didn't mind the walk. Mutti preferred for my sister and her friend to ride in a rickshaw, a sort of Pedicab with a seat on wheels and two long poles attached that was pulled by a coolie. Hongkou was a maze of alleys and streets. They were little girls, and the streets were constantly filled with the hustle and bustle of people. It's not like my parents were afraid my sister would be abducted or harmed, but the alleys were quite filthy, and there were sketchy areas, a lot of confusion. It was better if the girls were escorted from door to door.

I was reluctant to ride in the rickshaws. I didn't like the feeling of being carried by a person, of treating a person as if he were a pack animal, a horse. I sympathized for those poor fellows dragging a rickshaw behind them and running the entire way for a stick or a few pennies. The runners were all painfully thin. Skeletal. It was the way they made their living, but it was killing them. A conundrum. Starve without a job or run themselves down to skin and bones with it. Poverty in Shanghai was the landscape. Jewish hunger was a temporary situation. Chinese hunger was more permanent.

True, among us Jews, some kids had a little more food than others, but otherwise, there wasn't such a big discrepancy between the haves and the have-nots. We pretty much lived the same way. We went to the Kadoorie School. That wasn't its official name. The real name was the Shanghai Jewish Youth Association, but everyone referred to it as the Kadoorie School because it'd been financed by a man named Sir Horace Kadoorie. There were two Kadoorie brothers who'd made their fortunes in banking, rubber plantations, electric-power utilities, and real estate. Together, with the Sassoon family, they were the revered Baghdadi Jews, and without them, there would have been no school, no help, and for some, no food.

The Kadoorie School operated out of a building on Kingchow

Road that had originally been a Chinese college. It was run as if it were part of the British school system. The count of classes was One Upper, One Lower, Two Upper, Two Lower, and so forth. Lunch was called "Tiffin," and the warehouses were called "godowns." There were about seven hundred refugee children there. Classes were full. My teacher, Mrs. Christiansen, was from Shanghai, but she was of Norwegian descent. She only spoke English, not a word of German. For the first week, I stared at her blankly, but after the second week, I was able to differentiate sounds. A few days later, I started to hear words, and then, after three or four weeks, I could speak a little English.

English was the primary focus of our studies. It was assumed that we would all be immigrating to English-speaking countries as soon as possible. So Mrs. Christiansen would have us parse sentences. She'd write out a long sentence on the blackboard, and we had to identify the adverb, the subject, the adjective, etc. Grammar was the big thing. Among my friends and my family, I still spoke German, but at school, I had no choice. I learned English even if I spoke it with a thick Austrian accent.

After school, I either put my time in at Hebrew school, or more likely, I could be found playing football, meaning soccer, accruing my fair share of busted shins. Dinner at home was mostly kasha and caviar, both of which were very cheap in China. Red caviar was sold by Chinese vendors out of big vats, right on the street. It wasn't considered a delicacy since it was imported directly from Russia's Lake Baikal. We ate a lot of caviar, which was extremely salty. It made you thirsty, and that made you even hungrier. I was hungry for four years straight. I would have given anything for a chocolate sandwich. I would have eaten fat and loved it.

Often after dinner, a good friend of mine, Walter, would come get me, and we'd take a long walk around the jail, a large prison that consumed an entire city block smack in the center of the ghetto. As the war intensified, the front lines expanded beyond Europe, and air raids became a daily occurrence. The jail being the only reliably solid building in the neighborhood, it picked up double duty as a detainment center for British prisoners of war and the locals' largest bomb shelter. But for many years before those scary days, it was just the jail. The jail that held American gangsters who were let out for lunch every day under the escort of their paid-off prison guards.

Walter's father was a shirt maker, who, like Papa, believed his son should have a trade, just in case, a job to fall back on in the dark days, one never knew and certainly, we were living proof of life's precarious nature. It was understood that no matter how bad conditions became, the world would always need a tailor and a shirt maker. This was the shared belief of our fathers. Being sons, we saw things differently.

Every night, after dinner, the shirt maker's son and the tailor's son would meet for a long walk around a stone prison and vow to never sit in front of a sewing machine. After Shanghai, neither one of us ever did. Though, as it turned out, my knowledge of tailoring gave me a big advantage as a designer. So in the end, Papa was right. A trade was always a helpful thing to have.

Walter and I preferred instead to solve all the world's problems. When we walked and talked, we had all the answers. You wouldn't believe the things we solved. We rewrote history. We changed the future. Unfortunately, we had no tape recorder, so it was lost to posterity, but once we obliterated plague, pestilence, and starvation, our conversation could finally focus on the heart of the matter: girls. Neither of us had a girlfriend, and this was a matter of grave concern. The girls kept to themselves unless there was a group of kids together. There was no pairing off for dating, and of course, neither of us had any money anyway. Dating was a luxury we couldn't afford, and you certainly couldn't sneak your date into the movies. But talking about girls? That was free, so we indulged to our hearts' content.

At night, we fought the White Russians. They were the kids of the former Czarist officers, anti-Bolshevik Russians, and they were rabid anti-Semites. Their families left Russia during the revolution, along with many Russian Jews. It was the Russian Jews who ran the tailoring businesses in Shanghai. They hired Papa immediately as a fitter and patternmaker since he spoke Russian, and he had such a strong reputation in Vienna. Unfortunately, his reputation didn't protect me against the White Russians' sons. There were many fights between them and the Jewish refugee gangs. Every night, they hassled, fought, and chased us. I'd done a lot of running in Vienna. I did a bit more in Shanghai.

Still, I was unfazed by their pestering. To me, Shanghai was a great adventure. I thought I would live forever. It never crossed my mind I might die or be killed despite the fact that I saw people, Chinese and Jews, struggling to eat, make money, and stay healthy in the face of rampant poverty and disease. I was convinced I was immortal. Nothing could happen to me. Bad stuff happened to other people. Nothing could happen to my family. We were going to be fine. Papa had a job. He was a tailor. The world always needs a tailor.

SISTER

Everybody in class was more popular than me. My thick, red hair couldn't be fashioned into the little bottle curls that were in style. My hair went this way and that. It would not be tamed. The best Mutti could do was to stick a bow or a ribbon on my head and be done with it. She didn't have time to curl it. So the boys didn't notice me, and I didn't notice them. I didn't want to have a crush anyway because frankly, the boys were annoying. They were geeks though that word didn't exist then.

It didn't help that Papa made all my clothes out of remnants and blankets. We couldn't afford to buy new clothes from any of the major department stores: Sincere, Wing On, or The Sun. All of the department stores were fancy. They had restaurants or movie houses in them. The Sincere Company even used their entire ground floor as a tea hall. Among the four of them, Wing On was the most popular. It was a huge four-story emporium. On the ground floor, they sold cosmetics, knit goods, hardware, sweets, biscuits, canned food, and cigarettes. On the first floor, they offered silks and satins, piece goods, and clothing. The second floor was set aside for jewelry, watches and clocks, and musical instruments while the third floor sold furniture, leather suitcases, rugs, and bicycles. Their merchandise reflected their clientele; it was basically Chinese in character and for much wealthier people than us.

Those stores were terra incognita for the likes of us. In the ghetto, there were only a few mom-and-pop places; most of the buying was done at stalls, street markets that involved a lot of bargaining, which Mutti mastered as an art form. An Austrian Jew haggling in broken English with a Chinese vendor. Languages all around me.

As for our clothes, Papa could magically transform an old green army blanket into a coat with a hood. At first, I'd be embarrassed to wear such a coat until all my friends showed up wearing them, too. Papa started a trend. Our parents pretty much dressed us like babies even though we were ten years old. They wanted to keep us children not so much to feel youthful themselves, but more to retain our innocence. Maybe it was their futile way of clinging to the past or an attempt to stop time. Maybe they thought if we looked like toddlers, we wouldn't be able to understand what was happening around us. They infantilized us so effectively that some of us never grew up. The boys marched around in their shorts and knee-high socks. The girls, even the teenagers, looked like innocents. Normally, a teenage girl sees a boy, she gets ideas. She puts on earrings. Lipstick. Not us. There wasn't a slut among us.

I was extremely shy, painfully shy, remnants from feeling unwanted. I hated that every morning in school we had to stand up, say our first name, and then sit. I wanted to disappear into the back row of the classroom, but I was never lucky enough to be seated there. The teacher usually moved me closer to the front. She was a pretty woman, our lovely teacher, Miss Manessa, and everybody loved her, she was just darling. She used to choose one or two children to stay with her during the weekends since she lived in the French concession in a much nicer home than any of us. I wanted so desperately to spend the weekend with Miss Manessa, but she never picked me. I wasn't aggressive enough to be noticed. I didn't stand out. This is how I knew I had truly become invisible.

It was confirmed when we were cast for the school play to celebrate Purim, the story of Queen Esther. We reenacted the story of King *Ahasuerus* choosing his new queen, Esther, an orphan and a Jew. Raised by her cousin, Mordecai, Esther saves the Jewish people when she informs King *Ahasuerus* that not only is she Jewish, but his prime minister, Haman, intends to kill her cousin and her people. *Ahasuerus* instead orders Haman hanged on the gallows and allows Mordecai and Esther to write a decree that allows the Jews to defend themselves during attacks. There were all kinds of juicy roles in the play, but I got cast as a servant. My part was to stand there, silently, and fan the damn queen.

That damn queen was my best friend, Evelyn. She was the same age as me and lived across the street from us on Chusan Road near the Little Barcelona. She had those great bottle curls and was much more popular than me. Every morning, we took a rickshaw to school although some days, we'd only pay to ride halfway, and then we'd get out and walk the rest of the trip. We'd use the money we saved to eat street food, which was strictly forbidden by Mutti. She thought all Chinese street food was dirty, but the stores that sold water also sold the most wonderful oil sticks, and I craved them. The sticks were made out of flour and water and were braided into a long stick of dough that was then deep-fried in a big vat of boiling oil. Out would come this big, flaky pastry, the most wonderful thing to eat ever. It was greasy and delicious. The Chinese ate it with soup in the morning for breakfast because it wasn't sweet, it was bread. Mostly, I would sneak a single stick, but sometimes, on a real splurge, I would also buy a flat pancake. Similar to the braided dough, the pancake would expand when dropped into the oil. I would roll my oil stick into my pancake and eat them like a burrito. It was pure heaven. Those were exceedingly rare moments. Most of the time, I didn't have the money for such indulgences.

I went to school hungry. There were times I had nothing to eat except a couple of slices of bread I'd put on the classroom radiator to toast because they tasted better warm. That was lunch. You ate what you brought; they didn't give you a tray of food. I grew to resent the other children whose parents had more money or who owned a restaurant. They had no problem eating in front of us, the hungry kids, and not sharing. There was one girl whose dad had a grocery store. She brought food to show off, especially the popular raspberry drinks that were essentially red syrup water. She'd suck on her sugary drink as I choked down my radiator bread. It made me feel a lot better to think she was ugly.

As much as I liked my teacher, I hated school. I hated all the dictation and writing we had to do, and I really hated the gym teacher, Mr. Myer. He took particular pride in punishing me. The principal, Mrs. Hartwitch, was even worse. She was a big woman, solid, and she charged through the classrooms with an air of authority. Just hearing her name, everybody used to shake.

I was in a constant state of fear at school and at home. At school, I worried I would do something wrong and get hit. It seemed to me the teachers had a hitting quota they needed to reach each day, and if they didn't smack some kid around, they weren't doing their jobs. Then at home, I had to be a good girl, bathe myself in the basin, do my homework and stay superquiet so as not to upset Papa. If I was allowed outside to play with my girlfriends, I couldn't leave the block, and I absolutely could not play with the little Chinese girl that lived next door.

Mutti did not want Ilie or me to befriend anyone who was Chi-

nese. I didn't understand why. To me, a kid was a kid, and the little
Chinese girl that lived next door liked to play hopscotch. I was very
good at hopscotch. I'd had all that practice jumping over dead bodies. Me and the little girl, we'd hopscotch until Mutti would pull
me in, then I'd sneak out again, and we'd draw on the sidewalk with
chalk. Then Mutti would pull me in again, and we'd get creative and
play something that didn't make any noise at all. It didn't matter if
we were quiet as the wind. Mutti always found me and pulled me in.

She was afraid of everything and everyone. Her fear was omnipo-
tent even as she strained to appear stoic, to create the illusion of a
rosy life, a pleasant home. She couldn't hide her fear from me. I saw
her biting her knuckles. There was always a knuckle between her
teeth. It made me wish I was somebody else's child. I wished I was
Miss Manessa's daughter. I wouldn't just visit her lovely house on
the weekends. I would live there.

Hiding behind the red curtain in the closet, I fantasized. What
would it be like to be Miss Manessa's child? Or maybe, I was adopted.
Maybe my parents weren't really my parents, and I was the child of
a king or a queen. If I were the queen's kid, I would be the one lying
on a golden sofa being fanned. I would not be a servant. I would be
famous and very rich. Life would be so different. So much better. It's
not that I blamed my parents for our situation, but I could see they
were totally powerless, and I hated their powerlessness.

I wanted to spend all of my free time playing make-believe with
Evelyn. I wanted an escape that hiding behind a curtain in our
cramped room couldn't bring me. Evelyn and I, we'd pretend to be
a prince and a princess, dressing ourselves in all of our clothes and
acting as if they were costumes. We found a net on the street and
strung it up to make a tent. We were obsessed with becoming royalty. We'd seen an elaborate Indian wedding celebration between a
Jewish woman and an Indian man from the French concession. The
bride and groom were dressed in magnificent gold and white silks,
and the wedding party had actually thrown gold coins as part of the

procession. It was absolutely incomprehensible to me that money was being thrown into the streets, willy-nilly, as if it had no purpose, no value. Evelyn and I were thoroughly impressed by that display of wealth. We reenacted our own version of the decadence. Evelyn insisted on always being the bride even though I'd protest, "You were the bride last time!" She'd shrug and pretend not to remember, which is why I started hanging around with Miriam instead.

Miriam was a little bit older than me, and she sat at the end of my row in class. I liked her best of all because we could be more intimate in our conversations. Miriam talked about things other children wouldn't talk about like her parents divorcing. We'd climb onto the roof of my building and wonder aloud if we would ever grow breasts. We weren't sure at which age that was supposed to happen, and we were still little girls. Our parents hadn't explained anything. One day, Miriam announced she'd "grown one breast," which was quite shocking. We checked to see if it was true, but then decided she hadn't.

I talked to Miriam about my parents, too. Especially about Papa and his yelling. He yelled all the time. Not about anything personal, but just about life or people in general. In his opinion, everybody else was an idiot. Maybe compared to him they were. He had not one ounce of tolerance for stupidity. He cursed everything and everyone despite Mutti's useless attempts to calm him. I didn't like that Mutti was always so quiet and reserved. I wanted her to speak up, to say something, anything, just voice one thing she really disliked. She never did.

Miriam listened as I spoke words I never could have uttered in my own home. Like how I didn't understand the difference between being Chinese or Jewish or why my parents sent me to Hebrew school when Papa wouldn't even set foot inside a temple. It didn't make any sense. Why did I have to attend Hebrew school? Why did I have to celebrate the holidays by myself, without my family?

There'd been one happy holiday, they weren't all morbid, called Simchat Torah that had really upset me. Simchat Torah was a day to celebrate the reading of the last passage of the Torah with the reading of the first passage to follow immediately symbolizing the unbroken cycle of the Torah, a circle that never ends. There were processions, called Hakafot, around the synagogue with the rabbi carrying scrolls. There was dancing and singing, and all the children were expected to participate. We were given candied apples to eat and flags to carry. It should have been one of the happier days of my childhood.

Until I realized I was the only child walking around with a flag all by myself. All the other children had parents with them. It had all been Mutti's idea in the first place to send me to Hebrew school, but then she wouldn't come in. She would wait for me outside. She felt she couldn't participate because Papa was an atheist, and she needed to respect his ideals. She meant for me to be the continuation of her faith because without me, that aspect of her childhood upbringing would have died completely. I was the one who was supposed to keep it going, but I hated being there alone, the only kid without her parents, even on a happy holiday. Especially on a happy holiday. It made me feel as if my parents just wanted a place to keep me busy and out of their way once the school day was over. It reinforced in me the feeling I was unwanted. Not that I was able to express my frustrations so succinctly to Miriam. I just complained bitterly, announcing "school was stupid, and Hebrew school was even stupider." I knew standing on the roof and looking down at the bodies wrapped in white sheets, Evelyn playing alone in her net tent, and the little Chinese girl hopscotching on the sidewalk, Miriam understood what I meant. She was older. She had almost grown a boob. Miriam was a woman of the world.

BROTHER

The German freighter upon which all our furniture and Papa's equipment had been shipped was confiscated by the Germans. Mutti spent months and months speaking with lawyers (and anyone else who would listen) trying to track our possessions, but it was useless. Everything was gone. Mutti wept fiercely. It was one of the few times she allowed herself to break.

Papa, however, did not shed one tear. He already had a job with the Russian tailors as a patternmaker, then he found a client who wanted a suit made to order. A custom suit was good money. It could pay the rent and feed us for three weeks. Of course, to make a suit, Papa needed his sewing machine. We'd arrived in Shanghai virtually penniless and without any of the equipment Papa needed to run his own business.

Papa was not about to lose a customer for a "minor" detail such as no sewing machine. The war hadn't yet reached Shanghai, so fabric and thread and needles were easy to buy. Papa sewed the man's suit completely by hand. I watched as every stitch was meticulously rendered. Papa was a phenomenal tailor. The best. A master. The man who owned that suit never knew what a work of art he got.

Papa used the money from the suit to buy a sewing machine and supplies. He was back in business, using the tiny anteroom of our apartment as his shop. Customers were plentiful. I'd go with him to meet a customer, and before we'd walk into their apartments, Papa would nudge me and whisper, "Watch this. See how I do it." He had complete command of the situation. He always sold a suit. I was in great awe of him.

There was an enormous amount of money flowing through Shanghai prewar. People were working all over the city, some quite successfully, mostly those that lived in the French concession or the International Settlement. Shanghai had no extradition rights, so American gangsters moved in and made themselves at home. Everything in Shanghai was a payoff. Prewar, Papa did extremely well. His clients were wealthy Russians. Jews mainly served each other; there wasn't much crossover between Chinese and Jewish businesses though some Jews, like Papa, hired several Chinese tailors. Chinese tailors were fabulous craftsmen. Prevailing wages were so low, they hardly figured into the price of the garment. They were paid next to nothing for their time. The white man had a great life built upon the backs of the Chinese. It fed a well-deserved, anti-white sentiment among Chinese people and laid the groundwork for the Communist takeover. The white man didn't work at all, maybe three or four hours a day. The rest of the time was spent taking siestas to avoid the oppressive heat. All the Jews considered Shanghai a transitory place, a layover on the way to the United States. Businesses were opened in order to pay the rent and feed the children. Nobody had any intention of staying and building a whole new life in China. China represented a culture clash, and the older generation of Eastern European Jews could not acclimate. Figuratively speaking, they never unpacked. As the war in Europe dragged on, it became more and more clear we were stuck. A microcosm of European Jewish life began to form. An energetic and viable community emerged, and in the process, Hongkou was rebuilt. Two newspapers were published and distributed, an operetta company formed, a favorite Austrian diversion, bakers opened cafes and restaurants. In the heart of a vast Chinese city, a Jewish world emerged.

The cultural gulf was at its most visible, or rather audible, when attempting to cross the language barrier, in the difficulty of daily conversation. Since our knowledge of Chinese was nonexistent and the Chinese didn't speak German or Yiddish, we had to adopt a foreign tongue, English. Our command of English was rudimentary at best. Communication consisted mostly of pointing, gesticulating, and shouting. It was believed, by most, if you spoke louder, you would eventually be understood. Somehow, deals were made, groceries were sold, and Mutti and Dorit always came home from the market with a bag full of vegetables or kasha, never any meat. Meat was too expensive.

Petty animosities formed among us, certainly. Years and years of living on top of one another took its toll. It was not paradise, and even the angels fell from heaven. The German Jews looked down on the Austrians, and both looked down on the Polish as everyone went about their lives. But for the most part, there was cooperation among our people and the camaraderie that is created during hardship. There was no open animosity between the Chinese and Jews. We each had our own enemy and had suffered at their hands. There was an unspoken understanding formed from our mutual oppression that bred respect and pity between us. We were all struggling, no matter the color of our skin or language spoken.

Once I turned fourteen, I was expected to earn my keep so I left the Kadoorie School to attend business school where I was taught bookkeeping and stenography, which was then known as the Gregg System. I took the course for all of six months before it became apparent I was utterly useless in an office. I had to have a trade. It was a Jewish tradition. You had to be able to eat, and as a man, I had to be able to provide. I had to have some way to earn my keep.

So, despite all those walks around the jail with Walter declaring I would never sit in front of a sewing machine, Papa announced I would become a tailor. I was apprenticed to a tailor named Jellinek, a friend of Papa's, because I absolutely could not have apprenticed with my father. He was too strict, very demanding, we would have fought, and it would not have worked. Papa knew better than to put us through it. Jellinek was a patient teacher, and I learned quickly. My final exam was to make a suit jacket by myself from start to finish. I cut the pattern, lined it, sewed the seams, and finished the buttonholes. I passed my exam and received my diploma. I was a tailor.

Then the Japanese attacked Pearl Harbor, and everything changed. The Nazis began exerting pressure on the Japanese to do more about the "Jewish problem," but the Japanese were not anti-Semitic. In

1905, during the Russo-Japanese War, the Japanese had come to Europe looking for financial support. None of the European leaders would help because they were all related, in some way, shape, or form to the Czar. The Jews in those countries hated the Czar. They'd been driven out of Russia during the pogroms. The only money the Japanese were able to raise in Europe was Jewish money, and it was plentiful. The Japanese won the war, and they never forgot who funded their efforts.

That's the historical story. The apocryphal story says a Japanese commander sent for the head of the Jews. Since the Jews have no "head," they sent Amshinover rabbi Shimon Sholom Kalish. The Japanese commander wanted to know "Why do the Germans hate you so much?" Reb Kalish told the translator "Zugim weil mir senen Orientalim aseu wie ihr euchet." Translated, that means "They hate us because we are Orientals, like you." The commander, who had been stern throughout the confrontation, broke into a slight smile. It is said that because of the rabbi's response, the commander did not accede to the German demands, and the Shanghai Jews were never handed over.

Whether historical or apocryphal, the Japanese had no interest in rounding up Jews. They were busy hating the Chinese instead. On the Garden Bridge that divided the International Settlement from Hongkou, they posted two guards. White people could pass unmolested, but the Chinese had to bow. A sign hung on the entrance to the Race Course, a huge, beautiful public garden where soccer matches and races were held. That sign read "Dogs and Chinese not admitted." In the heart of their own city, the Chinese were treated as less than human.

As for us, the Japanese issued a proclamation to appease the Germans. The proclamation was called the Proclamation Concerning Restriction of Residence and Business of Stateless Refugees, and it was announced in every newspaper, posted on every wall. Word for word it read:

I. Due to military necessity, places of residence and business of stateless refugees in the Shanghai area shall hereafter be restricted to the under mentioned area in the International Settlement. East of the line connecting Chaoufong Road, Muirhead Road and Dent Road; West of Yangtzepoo Creek; North of the line connecting East Seward Road and Wayside Road; and South of the boundary of the International Settlement

II. The stateless refugees at present residing and/or carrying on business in the district other than the above area shall remove their places of residences and/or business into the area designated above by May 18, 1943. Permission must be obtained from the Japanese authorities for the transfer, sale purchase or lease of rooms, houses, shops or other establishments, which are situated outside the designated area and now being occupied or used by stateless refugees.

III. Persons other than stateless refugees shall not remove into the area mentioned in Article I without permission of the Japanese authorities.

IV. Persons who violate the proclamation or obstruct its reinforcement shall be liable to severe punishment.[1]

It was signed by the commander-in-chief of the Imperial Japanese Army and the commander-in-chief of the Imperial Japanese Navy.

Nowhere in the proclamation did it use the term "ghetto" or the word "Jew." In fact, Jews who had moved to Shanghai before 1938 were actually exempt. There were even stateless non-Jews who had to move. By pure luck, we were already living in the area that became formally known as the Restricted Sector. We didn't have to pick up and move again, but thousands of refugees did. It was already the poorest and most crowded area of the city, and then they squeezed

---

1 *Japanese, Nazis and Jews: the Jewish Refugee Community of Shanghai 1938-45* by David Kranzler (Yeshiva U. Press, 1976)

more people in without forcing the current Chinese residents to vacate. It became unbearable.

The Kadoorie School had to find a new facility. So Horace Kadoorie raised the money and built a new U-shaped, one-story building on Yuhang Road in the heart of what was now the Jewish ghetto. The building functioned not only as my sister's new school, but as my community center. He was able to get the building done just before all the Baghdadi Jews, the Kadoories and the Sassoons, were arrested and interned. Even the members of their staff from the I.C. were arrested. It nearly brought the Heime and the soup kitchens to a complete stop. Things got really hard, really fast. Nobody had any money or food except the Russian Jews who rallied to form the Committee for the Assistance of European Refugees. They did their best to continue the work of the I.C. and provide aid, but it became harder and harder to get money into Shanghai.

It also became harder to move around the city. A curfew was instituted and enforced by the pao chia, the Chinese name for a group of Jewish able-bodied men hired by the Japanese to act as a police force. Their presence created great fear that Jews were being organized to supervise and betray each other. Being a pao chia offered certain advantages. They wore armbands and wielded power over other refugees. They had more freedom. It was their job to patrol the borders of the restricted area, checking to make sure refugees were wearing their buttons and were not outside the ghetto after curfew. It was not a job that endeared them to their fellow Jews, particularly since it seemed to be taken more seriously than necessary.

The buttons or permits were issued by a Japanese officer named Kano Ghoya. He was a small man, about five-foot-five, with a little Hitler mustache, who strutted around and called himself "The King of the Jews." The lines outside his office stretched for blocks. Thousands of people lined up in the sweltering heat, in any kind of weather, so they could work. Everyone was afraid of him. He could be brutal, sadistic, and was clearly mentally unbalanced. He spit at people, was verbally abusive, and out of nowhere, he would jump onto the table and slap a man in the face. Especially if that man was tall. He had a Napoleon complex. He hated tall men.

If you were a student and you needed a pass to go to school, he might issue a pass that lasted two or three months. If you were an adult who had a job outside the ghetto, he might issue a pass that lasted one month or one day. His decisions were entirely arbitrary. His behavior was totally unpredictable. One day, he'd look at you and yell, "Two weeks," and the next time you came back, he'd yell, "No pass. Come back tomorrow!"

He worked in a medium of humiliation. His abuse was mostly verbal, though people did die if they were caught outside the ghetto without a pass. They were not beaten or killed. They were thrown into a prison rampant with typhoid fever, cholera, and dysentery. Because of their lack of resistance, it was often a death sentence. You'd get out, but then you'd only have a few weeks to live.

After the war, Ghoya claimed his abusive antics were just an "act," a persona created to satisfy the German authorities who were pressuring him to address the "Jewish problem" more forcefully. He claimed his actions protected us, and perhaps they did. For the entirety of the war, eighteen thousand Jews lived in enemy territory, surrounded, occupied, and ghettoized in the end, but the vast majority of us survived. In fact, the only European yeshiva to stay intact, the Mir yeshiva, did so because they fled to Shanghai. Whether or not Ghoya was responsible for our continued existence, I cannot say. I only know he made getting in and out of the ghetto an ordeal.

So much of an ordeal that work for Papa came in dribs and drabs; a coat to be reversed here, a pair of pants to be shortened or taken in so as to make for a better-fitting hand-me-down. Once in a great moon, a new suit would be ordered, and Papa would have me draw the jacket and pants in order to show the client. We didn't have access to magazines or catalogs, but Papa wanted his customers to see what they were getting in advance.

I'd sketch a handsome man with shortly cropped hair slicked back just so. I'd give him a strong jaw line and a confident smile. He needed broad shoulders and a narrow waist, the better to show off the masculinity of the jacket. Then Papa would specify whether it was a single-button lapel, a double-buttoned jacket, whether the pants were pleated, if they had pockets or a matching vest. My drawings of the models carried newspapers and walked with a bold stride. They kept their shoes beautifully polished and wore cuffed pants that hit just so. They had expensive watches, striped ties, and jaunty hats tipped at an angle. They had jobs in offices with a secretary to answer their phones. They did not have to show IDs to walk the street. They were Americans.

Papa's customers were always very impressed with my drawings, but it didn't make any sense to me that other people couldn't draw. I thought everyone should be able to pick up a pencil and draw a perfectly realistic man or train or Donald Duck.

My father recognized my talent even if I didn't and used it to help put food on our table. I was glad to be of service. I'd sketch, and suddenly, there was an order to fill and enough money coming in for us to eat for the next three weeks. Those orders were met with a great sigh of relief from Mutti. She worried incessantly, but Papa was the eternal optimist. "Who's going to worry? Three weeks! Something else will come again!" Something usually did, but mostly they were small jobs; hems and alterations. Our existence became very hand to mouth.

You'd think such circumstances would humble a man, but Papa was as brazenly stubborn as ever. He still treated customers as if they were nincompoops. He would not listen to even one word of criticism or even a question, so you can imagine the terror that ripped through all of our hearts when we learned the Japanese naval commander was coming to our apartment, with his cohorts, to have Papa make a suit.

Mutti implored Papa, "You have to be nice! You can't say anything to him!"

Papa shooed her away. "Yes, I'll be nice, I'll be nice."

The men arrived, and we cowered in a corner as far away as we could hide in our tiny apartment. As Papa measured the officer, we held our collective breath. The commander wanted one of their funny little suits with a high waist that came nearly to his armpits. We expected Papa to protest, "Absolutely not. You will have this in this fabric and cut like this," but he did not. Papa behaved like a gentleman much to our great surprise and relief. The commander was happy with his suit, and we had money enough for a month of eating.

The only other customers who could afford new suits were those who belonged to the Mir yeshiva, Polish religious Jews who were supported by Americans funneling money through Switzerland. They were the only ones with cash because most American relief organizations feared sending money would constitute trade with the enemy. The yeshiva students ate well when none of us ate at all. They may have had the ability to buy clothing, but they also had the habit of not trusting a tailor. When they arrived at our door, they always brought an entourage of "experts," friends to offer their opinions.

Papa would take one look at their crew and ask, "Who is getting the suit here?" A man would indicate he was the client, which caused Papa to wave his arms wildly and yell, "The rest out!"

A great protest would erupt. "What do you mean, out?"

Papa stood firm. "Only the person buying the suit can stay, and he has to be quiet!"

Mutti would bite her knuckles. We always needed the money, but Papa knew what he was doing. The entourage would leave, and the measuring would begin.

Most of his customers couldn't afford a new suit. Instead, they brought their old coats to have them turned inside out and made into "new" versions of themselves. Papa and I would take them completely apart, seam by seam. I was in charge of carrying the coats up to the roof and airing them out, cleaning every nook and cranny.

After ten years, all kinds of stuff collected in the hem of a coat or the armhole of the sleeve. It all had to be cleaned and brushed and shaken out as if they were musty old carpets from an abandoned house. Once I'd cleaned them thoroughly, I brought them back downstairs to the apartment where Papa would begin the real work of piecing them back together again. Humpty Dumpty style.

The fabric on the inside was like new, dark black most often, while its former exterior had faded gray. The only problem was the buttonholes ended on the wrong side of the coat once the material was flipped inside out. Those who could afford it had the buttonholes mended. The Chinese tailors had such fine, fabulous hands; they could mend a buttonhole so it looked like it never existed. Those with money to burn could even get the pocket flipped. Of course, for that, there was an extra charge, which led us to refer to those suits as "first class." Most of our coat repairs were "second class" with buttonholes and pockets landing on the wrong side of the suit.

These inside-out coats were our survival. We eked out an existence day to day. Then one day, there simply was no more money. A customer who was supposed to bring a suit in for alterations did not arrive. There was no food left. No money and no prospects in our immediate future. We had no choice. We had to pawn Mutti's wedding band. It fell upon me, this nasty task. It was inconceivable that either of my parents would risk the humiliation of being seen in a pawnshop, so I shrunk into my overcoat and hurried down the block, hoping against all hope that none of our neighbors would see me. To admit we were starving, to admit we needed help, these were not options. Even being seen at the Kitchen Fund carried a stigma. We could have gone there and had two hot meals a day, but being seen carrying a soup-kitchen pail of food was not an option. We had our pride. We needed to keep it intact. It was the only thing keeping us alive. Stubborn pride kept us going.

We weren't the only ones starving. The situation had become so dire that the rabbi lifted the prohibition against eating rice during

Passover because there was not much else to eat and rice filled the stomach. The sensation of hunger, of not knowing when food would come again, it was indescribable. There was nothing like it. Nobody should ever feel that hollowing emptiness. It narrowed all horizons. It created a singular focus of importance. Food, food, food.

Pawning Mutti's ring was the lowest we had fallen though I knew Mutti would not cry over it. In our family, sadness wasn't shown, though on the harshest of occasions, there would be weeping like when the Germans confiscated the ship that held all our belongings. Mutti wept over our lost history, over her collected memories, but I knew she wouldn't weep for a ring. Crying wasn't acceptable in our home. Lots of yelling, yes. But no crying.

My parents, their emotions played a single note repetitively: Papa played temperamental, and Mutti played stoic. Affection, love, sadness, melancholy, there was no room for the pendulum of emotion in our lives. No one ever said, "I love you." I never saw my parents so much as hug each other, though I assumed they were in love. They stuck together. They had a shared ancestry. They accepted life as it was. Their operating stance was survival. There was no questioning whether the marriage was "healthy" or "good for me." There was no "Who am I?" or "What will I be?" or "Why am I here?" No father needed to find himself. No mother felt oppressed. There was no angst despite the fact Freud was from Vienna. There was no crying over spilled milk.

And there were plenty of reasons to cry. With no food and living on top of each other and cockroaches so big they seemed to march in formation. Yes, there were plenty of reasons to cry. A pawned wedding band was not one of those reasons. So I slunk off to the pawnshop and handed over Mutti's tiny simple ring. I knew it was our last hope. The next morning, Papa's customer arrived at our front door and asked for his coat to be reversed. The crisis was over. We would be able to eat. I ran back to the pawnshop and happily redeemed my slip. I didn't care one smidge who saw me.

SISTER

I was too young to fully grasp the concept of war. What I was told and what I understood was this phrase "the bad people"—the bad people had taken over our country. Vienna was full of only bad people now. The good people had been forced out. They weren't allowed to live there anymore. The bad people were bombing America. The bad people were making trouble for everyone. I couldn't understand why someone didn't stop these bad people from being such a problem for the world. Who were these bad people, and why wouldn't they stop being bad?

I assumed this phrase "bad people" referred to soldiers, specifically Japanese soldiers. I'd gone with Papa to an office where white people lined up and waited for passes. Everyone in the line was very scared of a soldier they called General Ghoya. I heard whispered fragments, "Be sure he doesn't find out . . ." or "Don't say that . . ." People seemed eager to please him, and it was clear to me nobody had any intention of standing in front of his desk and telling the truth.

Mutti had been terrified of the Japanese soldiers when they came to our house so Papa could make the one in charge a new suit. She bit her knuckles and whispered to me, "Be very quiet. The soldiers are coming." She watched Papa so carefully, her hand over her mouth. I knew she was thinking, "They're going to kill us." Even Papa had let the soldiers stay. Normally, he threw everyone else out except the person getting measured. I knew if Papa let them stay, they must have been really, really scary.

All the Japanese soldiers carried themselves with such authority. The ones on the bridge made the Chinese people bow before continuing on their way. The ones in offices made white people scared. I developed a great fear of Japanese soldiers. I could spot their brown uniforms with the gold buttons and the orange rim of their hats from several blocks away. I didn't want to walk past them. I would cross the street if they were on my corner, or I'd go back home entirely.

I was terrified of their swords. They all had a sword on their hip, and they were constantly polishing the blades. The blades were long, about two feet, and they had a very pointy tip. They were shiny, and I could tell they had a razor-sharp edge. Some of the handles were ornately decorated, and some of the soldiers carried guns on their belts, as well. I was so terrified of those sabers, I could see nothing else.

I had good reason to hate those swords. In the park, I'd been playing with my friends, Judy and Peter, a pretty little boy with a girlish face, when a Japanese soldier approached and told us to pose for a photograph. They were forever taking propaganda photos of Jewish children to show we were clean, healthy, and happy. They scouted for kids that were photogenic to prove the ghetto was a humane environment. Peter had a pretty face, as did Judy. I had my freckles and fire-engine red hair held in place with my silly little bow. Compared to all the other children, the three of us were the best behaved. We didn't look like starving refugees. The photographer made Peter sit in the middle, and he told us to smile. None of us wanted to smile. There was nothing to smile about, we were sad kids, but we were afraid of the soldiers, so we smiled.

After the soldier took the photo, I noticed there was barbed-wire behind me. It was an area that was off limits, so of course, I wanted to explore it. I tried to climb over the wire, but it ripped my dress. A Japanese soldier saw me, and he walked over to me. He said something in Japanese indicating I shouldn't be climbing on the barbed wire, and then he unsheathed his sword. I held my breath as he poked the tip of the sword into my thigh. It pierced my skin. All I could feel was searing heat emanating through my leg. I tried to run away, but I got caught on the barbed wire, and that made the cut even deeper. I ran home bleeding.

Mutti took me to a doctor who sewed me up. I told her I fell at the park. I said not one word about the photographer or the soldier with his sword. I couldn't tell her what really happened. I was too afraid of getting in trouble. I was even more afraid Papa would hunt down the soldier who cut me. I didn't want to make Papa angry. I didn't want anything negative to happen to my family. I didn't want anything to do with the Japanese, and I didn't want to give the soldiers any reason to question us.

Life was dangerous, this much I knew, and it seemed to be getting more dangerous day by day. The Japanese soldiers were always around with their swords, but now they were joined by white policemen with armbands. Then suddenly our school had to move to a different building, and there were places we couldn't walk. Then we had to wear a button and be home at a certain time or else. I wasn't sure what the "or else" part meant, but I knew it was bad because the bad people were now in charge and getting meaner. I'd gone with Papa on a bus, and we'd been allowed to pass outside of our neighborhood because Papa had to measure a rabbi for a new suit. I kept looking around and wondering why we were the only ones who had to wear a button. Why were we being singled out?

I felt things should be fair. If someone did something good, I felt something good should happen to them. If I was polite, people should be polite back to me. I spent a lot of my youth proclaiming "it wasn't fair, wasn't fair"—nobody listened to me anyway. There was not much they could do about it. I didn't understand the lack of fairness I experienced in my daily life was directly related to our being Jewish. I just thought people were mean and a soldier might kill me, so I stayed close by Papa's side as we rode the bus and wished I had inherited his bravery instead of Mutti's anxiety. I was afraid of life.

It seemed like all the women who surrounded me, Mutti's friends and our neighbors, were equally as fearful. They spoke in complicated vagaries. They were vigilantly secretive. They divulged information on a pure need-to-know basis. They believed the words they spoke could be heard by the wrong ears, Japanese ears, German ears, by accident. They were distrustful even among each other.

The only woman who didn't behave so fearfully was Evelyn's mom. Her mom was referred to in whispers as a "loose woman." She was divorced even before Shanghai, and she lived with her mother and daughter. Three women living without a man raised eyebrows. She rode a bike, with her long, black curls flowing out behind her. She was youthful and scandalous, and she smoked heavily. The other moms gossiped about her, they said she "acted like a teenager," but I thought she was beautiful. I wanted to ride a bike with my hair cascading down my shoulders.

I just didn't have joy inside me. I'd seen too much death already. From the bodies wrapped in sheets to the four or five kittens we had tried, unsuccessfully, to keep as pets. Most of our neighbors had a cat or a dog as a pet, even if they were barely able to feed themselves. Adopting an animal brought a bit of levity into our lives. A pet kept you from thinking about what you didn't have, what you might never have, or what you already lost. Our neighbors upstairs had a dog they always kept on a leash, but I was deathly afraid of dogs. I'd been bitten once by a stray and had to get painful rabies shots, so dogs were out. Papa brought home kittens instead.

We had so many, they run together to create a composite of one extremely cute white kitten with a sweet face. Mutti would give it a spool of thread, and it would unwind the string, get tangled in the thread. I'd fall in love, get much attached, and then the kitten would die. Ilie became our family's designated mortician. We ran out of shoeboxes using them as kitty coffins. I stopped liking cats altogether. I didn't want to pick up a kitten and feel its heartbeat. I didn't want to pet its warm fur. Touching the kittens started to burn my hands. I couldn't get my hand away fast enough.

BROTHER

Once America declared war on Japan, Papa felt certain the war would not last much longer. Mutti and her friends daydreamed about leaving Shanghai. Dorit asked my parents every day, "When are we leaving for America?" Our hopes were raised. My friends and I, we became military experts, strategists, cartographers. We listened to the radio religiously. We became voracious readers and could speak with authority about the historical context of a battle, the borders that were changing hands, the major players, and the geography of the world. We might have been teenage boys, but we knew enough to ask questions. We remembered our homelands. We knew we'd been shoved out. We remembered boarding the ships and arriving in China. We wanted vengeance.

We got our news from the German papers. The ghetto papers were apolitical. They could not print content that might upset the Japanese, so they functioned as glorified social pages: announcements, marriages, upcoming cultural events, and slice-of-life stories. Now, the German paper had a German agenda, but we could still gauge the progress of the war by reading between the lines. When the Germans advanced in Russia, the newsprint read, "Previous territorial gains retained." We knew it wasn't going well.

We began to lose all of our newly won hope when Japan swept through the Pacific, conquering Burma, the Dutch East Indies, and Singapore. It was incomprehensible they'd captured Singapore. Singapore was British. We'd been so certain it wouldn't fall, but the British had ordered defenses to face the sea, and the Japanese had invaded through Burma, coming by land. The news was terrible. There were heavy casualties, severe losses, and a large number of prisoners taken. The Japanese went on to conquer the Philippines, bombed Australia, and claimed naval victories in the Indian Ocean. The mood in the ghetto darkened, quite literally. All our windows had to be covered to create a blackout, and the already miserable conditions deteriorated.

Air raid sirens filled the air. First, we'd hear the planes in the distance, on the outskirts of Shanghai. The Japanese had ammunition holdings out there. We'd hear those big planes, and then BOOM, BOOM, BOOM, we'd hear the concussion of the bombs dropping and landing. Only then would the sirens in Shanghai sound. We were all supposed to run to the prison and take shelter in its basement, but the air raids happened so often, we stopped running for shelter and started looking up at the sky. Those American bombers would buzz over us, and I could see the glint of metal in the clouds. They were much more impressive than the paper planes I used to send reeling off my terrace in Vienna. Paper planes were child's play. This was war. I hoped the Americans were zooming over Vienna and terrifying the Germans. I stood in the streets and cheered them on.

With the war literally hanging over our heads, we went about our lives. Theaters kept putting on plays; restaurants kept their doors open; and a black market flourished, providing supplies at exorbitant prices. There were wheelers and dealers who knew how to maneuver, and even at the height of the war, there wasn't a thing you couldn't get in Shanghai if you had the money and were willing to risk imprisonment. Coca-Cola went for ten dollars a bottle. My family's limited funds paid for rent and food; everything else was a luxury.

My friends and I spent most of our time at the new Kadoorie School, which also functioned as the Jewish community center. There, we played ping-pong for hours and came to fancy ourselves as "pretty good" until an informal tournament with some Chinese players put us in our place, fast. They killed us. There was no comparison. Ping-pong was in their genes. It served as a wonderful distraction between waiting for the newest edition of the paper. It was like being on that Italian luxury liner and not knowing where, in the open sea, we actually were and every morning, waiting anxiously for a sailor to stick a red pin in a map so we could reorient ourselves. The German newspapers with their propaganda and their bravado functioned like red pins in a map, charting our progress, signaling our coordinates. Our fate in the hands of a larger force, the governments of the world instead of the ocean.

And finally, the tide began to turn. The first headlines read, "Heavy Casualties Inflicted on American Invaders," and we took that to be a good sign. They had called the Americans "invaders," which meant there had been an invasion of some sort—an offensive move and the accompanying article had not mentioned one word about forcing a retreat. Then rumors filtered in saying the Americans were taking back the islands, and the German troops at Stalingrad had been forced to surrender. People's spirits lightened. Everyone became a bit more optimistic. Even if fighting between the Chinese and the Japanese had intensified, the Allies were gaining momentum. It never even crossed my mind the war could actually touch Shanghai directly. That our lives might be in danger.

SISTER

Ilie spent a lot of time sitting by the window, drawing, in his usual spot. He liked to sketch the activities of the Little Barcelona, the women standing around, the guys drinking. He drew what he saw in the streets. Beggars and babies, old men carrying big loads on their backs. He was sitting there drawing when everything started to shake.

We heard the planes before we saw them, and I could tell they were American planes. American planes were like a bullet, *buzzzzzzzzzzzzzzzzzzzzzzzzz*, while Japanese planes were squeaky and clumsy sounding. Mutti yelled at both of us, "Get downstairs!" but Ilie wouldn't budge, he wasn't finished with his drawing. We could see the planes. They were only a few blocks away. Mutti yelled at him again, "Ilie! Now!" but he kept drawing. He was trying to capture the moment in charcoal. As the bombs began to land, he kept drawing.

The impact. I felt the vibrations through the earth. Buildings exploded. The sirens and the screaming and the sound of destruction. Hell. It was indescribable. We started running, down the stairs, down to the basement of our building. Cowered there. Waited for the bombing to stop. Suddenly, it dawned on me things could get very, very bad. Much worse than they had been.

The bombing stopped. I'd been given lessons through the Red Cross. I put on my white cap with the identifiable red cross stitched on it. I grabbed my bag, full of bandages, and ran out into the streets with my brother. The whole neighborhood had rushed to help. Parents and children alike. I was ten years old, but I had to be of use. I had no choice about it. I had to grow up fast in case I didn't grow up altogether.

The bombs were dropped from American planes. The sky had been solidly overcast making the visibility of their targets impossible. They were trying to hit a radio station, but they couldn't see anything. They based their drop on their flying time. Two hundred and sixty-three bombs dropped on Shanghai. Each of the bombs weighed one hundred pounds. They landed on the market.

It felt very personal to me, the annihilation of the market. Mutti and I spent a great deal of our time there since food, when we had the money for it, had to be bought on a daily basis. When Mutti bought eggs at the market, she made the vendor hold the egg up and shine a flashlight through it before she'd buy it. The market was always packed with people, pushing and shoving their way around. There were pickpockets, so Mutti always carried two wallets, one empty and one full. If she suspected someone was targeting her, she showed them the empty wallet, and they'd go away. The market was my home away from home.

The devastation was incomprehensible. Men ran past dragging rickshaws, pedaling pedicabs transporting the injured. There were fire trucks and ambulances, arms and legs scattered among the debris. I saw a man with half his foot hanging off and the other foot missing entirely. I thought I was supposed to figure out where his foot went. Ilie immediately began helping to pile the dead bodies, but I ran around handing out bandages until they were gone. I wasn't scared or disgusted. If someone had told me to bandage a man's leg back to his body, I would have done it. I wouldn't have thought twice about it. I was only ten.

Two hundred and fifty people died that day in the market. Thirty-one of them were Jewish. The rest were Chinese. Another five hundred were injured. The rest of us, we were "lucky"—just scarred for life. I still have the charcoal drawing Ilie made during the bombing. It hangs on my wall. If I really stop to look at it, the fear of that day is freshly conjured as if the miles from San Francisco to Shanghai do not exist. As if the years between the little girl I was and the woman I am today never passed, and if, in the background, I happen to hear a police siren or an ambulance zooming past my building, I still shake. I shake, and I shake.

BROTHER

There were ugly rumors spreading through the ghetto that all the Jews would soon be shipped away. People said there were large boats waiting in the ports to be used for our transport, and if we boarded them, we would be killed. The Japanese dug foxholes and trenches in front of each house, prepping to defend Shanghai against American troops. Tensions rose. Everyone was apprehensive.

There were two plans, one by General Stilwell and one by General MacArthur. MacArthur's plan was to attack Japan by sea, island hopping, going from island to island, and then launching a direct attack on Japan proper. The Stilwell approach was to move up the coast of China and then attack Japan. If Stilwell prevailed, there would be fighting in Shanghai. None of us would survive. If MacArthur prevailed, we would most likely be safe.

Then on July 17, 1945, I will never forget the date, American bombers made their usual noon appearance, high in the sky. Only this time, instead of flying over, they opened their cargo doors, and bombs fell like rain. Until that moment, despite all our hardships, I had considered myself a spectator of the war, staring out my window, drawing the life below. As the ground shook and Mutti screamed for me to "Run!" It occurred to me I might not be around to see what happened next. The war was once again at my front door, and this time, Alois could not protect us. Bombs were even more dangerous than boots.

Once again, luck was on our side. Dorit and Mutti had not gone to the market that day. Papa was out of the ghetto, visiting a customer. My family survived the bombing even if we were not spared its horrors. Like everyone else, we ran into the streets to help. Chinese or Jewish, it did not matter. We bled.

Less than a month later, there was a small article in the paper saying that two big bombs had exploded over some Japanese cities. Then suddenly, one morning, we woke, and the Japanese were gone. In the middle of the night, they had completely disappeared. The police station was empty. The bridge guards were gone. No more soldiers roaming the streets. For two days, there was complete confusion, but miraculously, no looting. Then we heard the amazing news. Japan had surrendered. The war was over.

There was much jubilation in Hongkou. Within a few weeks, American soldiers started to arrive. The first wave of them, pilots. They drove through the streets in Jeeps and drank beer at the Little Barcelona. These were the same pilots who had dropped the bombs on the market. I asked them, "Didn't you know there was a ghetto below you?"

They claimed they had poor visibility, a cloudy day.

I pushed back, "So why not dump the load in the Pacific Ocean?"

Then the Seventh Fleet of the American navy came ashore. They hadn't set foot on dry land in more than four years. It was chaos. Immediately, there was food. Rations were handed out, and they were the tastiest meals I had ever eaten. I was filled with a tremendous sense of freedom, and for the first time in years, I wasn't hungry.

Our ghetto was officially liberated on September 3, 1945. The

Americans allowed Chiang Kai-shek's army to take credit for our liberation. They flew the Chinese soldiers in so they could march through the streets. The Chinese soldiers were wearing straw sandals tied around their legs with ribbons. Some were wearing uniforms, but most weren't, and only a few of them had rifles. It was a far cry from the regimented, well-equipped, goose-stepping parade I'd witnessed in Vienna. They didn't look like a real army much less our liberators, but we cheered them anyway.

The entry of U.S. troops brought the full details about that tiny article in the newspaper. Two atomic bombs had been dropped over the cities of Hiroshima and Nagasaki. My mind could not possibly understand the magnitude of the destruction, even after witnessing the devastation of our market by much smaller, less-powerful bombs. Nuclear weapons were incomprehensible. To hear that entire cities no longer existed, that hundreds of thousands of civilians had died. It was too much.

Then we got word about the Holocaust. Though there had been rumors, speculative murmurings prior to our liberation, most of us had heard nothing from relatives for years. The soldiers talked about extermination camps, death marches, gas chambers, and mass graves. The jubilant mood inspired by our liberation quickly quieted. A deep sorrow swept through the streets, touching every life. General Eisenhower had visited one of the concentration camps and was so outraged, he sent reporters, photographers, and filmmakers to document the atrocities. Explicit photographs appeared in Life magazine, newspapers carried the images. It took a while for us to see those images, but they made it to us eventually. Everything we'd been through suddenly paled in comparison. The hunger, the disease, the curfews, the poverty, none of it mattered anymore. We were lucky. Nobody gassed us. We had our lives, but that was no cause for celebration.

Mutti began searching for her sister's family, sending letters, scanning lists of the dead, the found, the survivors. There was much confusion. European refugees were being shipped to displaced-persons camps, DP camps, which were being run by the United Nations, but then other international refugee organizations like HIAS, the Hebrew Immigrant Aid Society and the Joint were also helping out. There were multiple lists of names circulating at any given time. These were "grown-up matters," which meant my sister and I heard only bits of information. We were not given the whole story.

It took months for Mutti to learn her sister and her sister's family had all died at Dachau. Only her sons had survived. The ones who fled before the Anschluss. The youngest, a water-polo player for the Vienna Hakoah, had stayed in the United States with his team and all the women swimmers who boycotted the Berlin Olympics. The Austrian government considered their actions an affront, but neither the swimmers nor the polo players relented. They stayed in New York.

This proved to be a big bone of contention with the eldest brother who fled Austria, his journey much less glamorous. He paid a guide to sneak him and his wife into France. They were caught and separated, but miraculously found each other again in Marseilles, which was not yet occupied by the Germans. They had the good sense to get out of there quickly and made their way to Switzerland where the guards at the border could be paid off. They bribed a specific guard, but the night they were meant to cross, he was stationed elsewhere. They were turned away. They hid for two more days until their guard returned, and they were able to cross into safety.

Both brothers had escaped with their lives, but there was bad blood between them. The eldest believed the youngest had abandoned his family; he hadn't done enough to help get his family out of Vienna. What he'd been able to do or hadn't done didn't matter. Mutti's sister and the rest of her family were murdered, and Mutti wept.

SISTER

The first American I ever met was a sailor. The ships came in bringing with them sweets and candy, chocolate bars and Juicy Fruit chewing gum. I could not have cared less about the handsome sailors handing me packets of red Jell-O. I just wanted to eat the sugary powder straight out of the box. I didn't know you were supposed to cook it.

My girlfriend, Miriam, was always ahead of her time, and she wanted to go to the ships to meet one sailor who was "really nice." She said he would give us chocolates. I snuck off to go with her. I couldn't tell my parents. I was strictly forbidden to go near the ships, but I really wanted chocolate, and Miriam swore he was nice, so I went. The soldiers were very rowdy. They picked Miriam up and pretended they were going to throw her in the ocean. It scared me so bad I ran all the way home.

With the Americans came an influx of new American movies, which made me happier than any old box of Jell-O ever could. For the entirety of the war, we'd been stuck with films that would never leave. Usually they were the Tarzan movie or serial movies like one of the chapters from Flash Gordon. We had to wait forever for the next film to make it to Shanghai, so they'd just show the same movie over and over and over again. Flash driving off the side of a cliff. I never got to see how he survived that calamity.

I got so desperate for new entertainment I began sneaking into Chinese movies even though I couldn't understand a word. Ilie wouldn't sit through them, but to me, it was still a movie. The Chinese films always started with the Chinese national anthem, and after a while, I heard the anthem in my head everywhere I went.

The Chinese actresses wore heavy makeup with lots of trinkets in their hair. They were so heavily made up, I couldn't tell which actress was which. They wore long dresses and had tiny, perfect figures. The male actors were ugly. I didn't like any of them. The stories themselves were operas, completely sung through, with those nasally, high-pitched tones that sounded, to my foreign ears, like squealing. The actor would press himself against the actress, and they'd sing like that with half an inch between their lips, singing right into each other's faces. They would almost kiss, but then they wouldn't, and they would part, looking at each other, forlornly. You never got to see them kiss. It drove me nuts. I wanted him to just grab her by the hair and kiss her and be done with it.

There were two movie houses near our apartment in Hongkou, both of them cesspools. The floors were covered with urine, spit-out sugarcane and sunflower seeds, the snacks of preference for the Chinese who came to see films. Mutti never let me eat the sugarcane, which came in long stalks, five or six feet long that were cut up into smaller portions, chewed up, and then spit out with no concern for where the spittle landed. Ilie was forever wiping spit off the back of his neck during a movie. It had nothing to do with his being Jewish. If he'd been Chinese, the same thing would have happened.

I tried once to eat sunflower seeds the way I saw Chinese men doing it. They could put a whole handful of seeds in their mouths, separate the seed from the shell with their tongues, and then spit out the shells, poot, poot, poot. I put a bunch in my mouth and just about choked to death trying not to swallow them whole. Ilie preferred the pomegranates.

It was a disgusting place to spend time, but I went over and over and over again, and once the Americans landed, I could go there, curl up in my seat (careful to keep my feet off the urine-soaked floor), and listen very carefully to the GIs sitting behind me, making out with their new girlfriends, whispering promises in American, which sounded a little bit like the English I'd been taught, but not really. I strained to hear them because American is what I wanted to speak. America is where I wanted to be.

I had to get to America because everyone in America had a pool. I knew this because I'd seen Bathing Beauty. In fact, I'd seen it over and over again. I knew it by heart. First, the actresses started by dancing. There was a trumpet solo, then the band would kick in, and the girls in their long, pink flowing gowns swayed and swooned over a series of stairs, waving their arms back and forth, their gorgeous reflections mirrored back to them on the glassy surface of the untouched pool. It drove me crazy when they danced. I just wanted them to dive in, headfirst and let the cool waters transform them into mermaids. Dance they would until finally, they'd form what looked like a kick line, and I'd sit tall in my seat so I could see over the head of the kid in front of me as the women took off those flowing robes to reveal their pink-and-green, sparkly bathing suits, and the music trilled, and the camera pushed toward them and they fell like dominos, one by one by one by one, gracefully sideways into the pool, and now, the movie really started to get good.

The drums thumped faster, and the swimming girls clapped then flipped, clapped then flipped, and those unfortunate dancers, the ones who had to stay on the stairs, started to shimmy and spin, and I knew, soon, soon she would appear. Yes, yes, the music shifted, and the dancers gave way as from below the stairs ascended a platform that held two huge seahorses and in between them stood the most beautiful woman I'd ever seen in my life, aside from my mom, of course. That woman was Esther Williams.

Esther was a Greek goddess in her chiffon white cape and her bejeweled, belted tunic with her perfectly coiffed hair held tightly to her head with what surely must have been diamonds. Women in flowing yellow, blue-and-black dresses quickly flitted about her, helping her to elegantly disrobe until she was wearing only a shiny, silver bathing suit that hugged every curve so tightly I had no idea how she could breathe out of the water let alone under it. Everything about her sparkled, the diamonds in her hair, the jewels on her suit, her smile, even her skin was luminescent.

And then she started to run. Even I knew you weren't supposed to run by a pool, but she ran down the stairs, and I didn't care that

I might trip and fall, I wanted to run with her. She ran toward the refreshing pool. She ran because she could no longer stand dry land, she ran because she knew the water was her home, because she truly was a mermaid, and even two seconds on the screen in the middle of a hot, stifling theater in Shanghai was two seconds too long. She needed the water. She needed the pool. In the pool, she was free.

She dove, and every single time, I inhaled sharply and held my breath and tried to hold it for as long as she'd stay under, but I couldn't. She was part fish—of this I was certain. I watched wide eyed as she'd emerge, back on the surface, still smiling, not even breathless, and the long legs of the swimmers surrounding her would flutter and kick up a whirlpool of bubbles, then with a few strokes transform into a circling flower, spinning loops, twirling and flipping as Esther slithered among the underwater melee, her eyes open and not even squinting like any normal person would. Not even a little bit.

Then, in a climactic tour de force of Hollywood proportions, Esther resurfaced as jets of water burst into the air, spraying fountains that shot sky-high, water falling like rain, but that wasn't enough. Flames of fire were thrown heavenward in a mad crescendo of music, fire, and water as Esther took her rightful place on a platform that rose out of the pool, swimming girls spinning and kicking and genuflecting around her as she lifted her arms and posed and glowed with beauty. Esther Williams was glorious.

I applauded every single time.

They made amazing fodder for daydreaming, the Esther Williams movies. After seeing her on the big screen, I would run home, hide behind the curtain, and practice lounging by my washbasin as if it were a pool. I'd pretend a maid had brought me a milkshake, and I was dressed in frilly clothes, gorgeous clothes, with lace and organdy and tulle. I imagined I would take my dinner dressed as such, and the servants would serve me, but I'd be good to them. I would allow them to sit at the table and eat with me because they were just like me, just a little bit older, like my parents, and we'd all join together and become a big, happy family of aunties and uncles wearing long, formal dresses to dine.

My God. My God. Why were we still living like rats?

BROTHER

The United States Armed Forces became a large presence. They paid handsomely, so most of my friends took jobs with the Navy, driving the trucks. Papa's business was up and running again. He no longer needed me as a tailor. When my friend, Bob, left his job as a file clerk at the Joint, he passed it on to me.

The "Joint" was what we called the American Jewish Joint Distribution Committee. They were in the business of helping Jews all over the world. They'd been in Shanghai before Pearl Harbor, but once the U.S. entered the war, they were no longer legally permitted to operate within an enemy country. Shanghai was considered the property of the Japanese making the Joint a bit handcuffed. Once the ghetto was liberated and the Americans were in charge, the Joint returned full force to help resettle refugees and get food, medicine, clothing, and supplies from the United States directly into our hands. The man heading their efforts in China was Charles H. Jordan.

Mr. Jordan was an American, born in Philadelphia. He'd been educated as a social worker and then served in the army before joining the Joint and becoming the far-eastern representative for the JDC. He was in his forties when I met him. He was short, broad shouldered, and fastidious. He smoked cigars. He wore glasses, clean white shirts, double-breasted suits, rep ties, and his hair combed straight back. He was a brilliant speaker. His thoughts flowed easily. He spoke for hours without a note of any kind. His grammar was flawless. He impressed me greatly. He impressed everyone.

He was an idealist and a profoundly decent man who clearly had to be tough as nails. He was dealing with international governments, world leaders, and the bureaucracy of resettling stateless refugees from far-flung corners to Israel. Still, he always spoke with such thoughtfulness it seemed to me he truly loved his work and believed in his purpose. It was inspiring just to be around him.

We first met when a Jewish army chaplain, Rabbi Fein, and a Jewish army welfare worker, Harry Herbert, united with Mr. Jordan to help us boys form a club called Tikvah. I'd taken Bob's job as a filer at the Joint, and I was terrible at it. Not wanting to fire me, my boss found something else for me to do. He knew I could draw, so he asked me to start a newspaper for the Jewish teenagers. I became the editor in chief of Jewish Youth. I wrote, illustrated, and mimeographed it. My humble paper came to the attention of those three men who essentially volunteered me to become a founding member of their new club, Tikal, with my friend, Bob, stepping in as president. It became a very successful social organization where many close friendships were forged including a lifetime bond with "Charlie," as we boys affectionately called Mr. Jordan.

Our first order of duty was to put up a production of Arsenic and Old Lace. Charlie wasn't as interested in my capabilities as a theatrical producer as he was my art. He saw my drawings in the youth paper and marveled at their realism. I offered to make a drawing of him. It was the drawing that changed the rest of my life.

Because getting out of Shanghai was turning out to be harder than we'd hoped. Everyone who'd been able to secure visas prior to the war had priority. Their paperwork was already in order. They were first in line. Second in line were the rabbinical students of the Mir yeshiva, not because the Joint decided they took precedence, but because they were all Polish citizens and students and not technically stateless. They had a home country. They were able to get their passports back, and American yeshivas arranged for them to get visitor visas. The rest of us, we were still stateless. We could get visitor visas to the United States, but we had to prove there was an end destination. Once again, we were trapped by bureaucracy.

Then Mr. Jordan saw my drawing. He studied it carefully, thoughtfully and asked me quite earnestly, "Ilie, would you like to study art in Paris? I can get you a scholarship at l'École des Beaux Arts." Would I ever! I didn't hesitate for even one second. "Yes!" Yes. Yes. Yes. Mr. Jordan tried to slow me down, ground me in reality. "It would mean you'd have to leave your family, and it could be for a long time. It's chancy." But the opportunity to be an artist was simply too seductive. I impressed upon him my commitment. "I want to go."

I rushed right home and told my parents Mr. Jordan was going to send me to Paris. He'd already helped Bob get into Columbia University's School for Social Work. He'd helped a very talented violinist get to the United States. It wasn't even his job to get us into schools, but he was doing it. On his own. He saw potential in me, and he didn't want it to go to waste. He believed in my talent.

My parents met with Charlie to discuss my future. They trusted him instantly. Papa, in particular, was wowed, which was a feat in and of itself, but Charlie was quite a charismatic man. My parents had no reservations. There was no argument at all. Papa was absolutely determined to help Charlie get me to Paris, and it wasn't like I had to be pushed out the door. Paris was a big deal, but I would have gone to Mongolia if it meant I could study art.

Charlie's JDC headquarters were in Paris. He promised he would write to me once he got home and had secured the scholarship. True to his word, he did. He gave me one last shot to back out. "Do you still want to come to Paris?" My answer was an unequivocal, "yes!"

I was seventeen years old.

SISTER

I wanted so desperate to get out of Shanghai and move to America that I pestered Mutti daily about it. Every day, she promised me,

"Tomorrow. We're leaving for America tomorrow." I lived on those tomorrows. Waiting and waiting for them to come true, and then, tomorrow came. Just not for me. Ilie was going to Paris.

A short round man with dark hair and dark-rimmed glasses came to our house. He was pretty much the same shape as Papa, but not nearly as loud. He talked about Ilie's talent and his education, and by the end of the talk, it was all decided and done with not one complaint from Papa. Mutti seemed to be in a state of shock. With all she'd seen and having lost her entire family, she knew there were no guarantees. If Ilie left us, it was entirely possible we would never see him again, but Papa must have felt it was a chance to save Ilie, to at least save one of us. One of us had to get out. Ilie got a copy of a French dictionary and started memorizing words.

As for the three of us, Mr. Jordan wanted us to consider resettling in Palestine. Papa hated the idea of a kibbutz, communal living in cramped quarters with no independence. He didn't see a difference between the Shanghai ghetto and a Jewish kibbutz except everyone involved would be Jewish instead of Chinese. He was an atheist, and he didn't want to be involved, and he certainly didn't want to move somewhere where enlisting in the army was mandatory. In a kibbutz, they toughened you up real quick. It would have been like hopping out of the frying pan and into the fire. If Kibbutz Galuyot was our only option, we were staying in Shanghai. Papa was a stubborn, stubborn man.

He also became super strict when it came to my eating. We'd been without food for so long, he insisted I eat every morsel on my plate at every meal. I'd had a taste of those American sweets and candies, and that's all I wanted. I didn't want to eat Mutti's goulash and dumplings with the prunes inside. I hated lettuce, and Mutti was forever serving us salads of lettuce, tomatoes, and onions covered with some sort of oil. Even when she tried to teach me how to make potato dumplings, rolling the dough and filling it with potatoes, cream cheese, and onions, I wasn't interested. Papa's solution was to make me wear my coat at dinner until I cleaned my plate. The summers were brutal, horribly hot, 105 degrees with full humidity. So hot you'd try not to move so you wouldn't drip sweat. At night, I'd suffer as long as I could under the blanket to keep from being bitten by bugs, but I'd get too hot and have to kick it off. So wearing a coat to dinner was unbearable. I choked down the dumplings.

I was absolutely miserable. All around us, people were leaving. The rabbis and the rabbinical students had their visas. Older girls from my school tried to marry them quickly in order to get out. I didn't understand why religious people were receiving preferential treatment. It seemed unfair even though fairness had never been part of my life's equation. I watched bitterly as month after month, fewer and fewer friends remained. I didn't feel their leaving as deeply as I thought I would, having spent so many years as their neighbor or classmate. It was only when Miriam and Evelyn left that I truly felt the crushing impact of loss. I'd been extremely close to them both. I felt abandoned.

Papa's old desertion was causing us a few problems, but in reality, it was Papa who was the big problem. Early on, right after our liberation, New Zealand offered to take artisans, tailors being included in that category. Everyone was so jealous of us, and I got excited. It wasn't America, but we were still getting out. Papa wouldn't go. Then Australia eased their restrictions, and a ton of refugees headed down under. Not Papa. "It's a land of convicts!" He just would not budge.

On the day Ilie left for Paris, the four of us gathered in the yard outside the U-shaped Kadoorie School and posed for a family photo. It was never said aloud it might be the last time we were all together, but I was worried. The four of us stood in a line. My parents put on their brave faces, sorrow in their eyes. As if a Japanese soldier was forcing them to smile for a propaganda camera. Ilie and I both reached in and locked arms with our parents who kept their hands tucked into the pockets of their coats, all of our clothes made by Papa. It's the closest we ever came to a group hug.

P_{ART} *III*

PARIS, NEW YORK, MONTREAL

BROTHER

Getting to Paris wasn't as easy as jumping on the next plane. Charlie may have gotten me a full scholarship at l'École des Beaux Arts, but there was still the issue of me being born stateless. In order for the French government to issue me a student visa, I had to have an end destination. A place I could return to after my studies. A student visa did not entitle you to stay in France forever, and I certainly wasn't going back to Shanghai. I had to become a citizen of some country, or more accurately, I needed to look as if I was already a citizen of a country. Charlie worked his magic one more time. Ecuador gave me a document certifying that after my studies in Paris, I could live there. It was entirely bogus, but it was enough to secure the French student visa. Charlie also secured a visitor's visa for the United States, giving me four weeks to see New York before I settled back in Europe.

I stayed with cousins in Washington Heights. The image I had of New York was exactly the city I found. I loved the whole place even if the subway was beyond intimidating. I'd just gotten the hang of it when it was time to start school. As I boarded the *Queen Mary*, the ship's officer looked at me strangely. A redheaded Jew with a Chinese stateless passport, a French student visa, and an Ecuadorian end document. I shrugged, "It is what it is!" and we had a good laugh. The journey across the Atlantic lasted seven days. I slept in third class, but I played ping-pong in first. I knew no one on the boat, but ping-pong makes friends fast. I had a great time. I spent my first two nights in Paris at a hotel near Montmartre. It turned out to be a bordello with men coming and going all night. It was a good introduction to Paris.

Charlie quickly moved me into a boarding room let by a Russian-Romanian Jewish widow. She was a beautiful woman and a Stalinist. In the morning, we'd have breakfast together. She'd read *l'Humanite*, a Communist paper, and I'd read *Le Monde*, the complete opposite. She'd point to her front page, "Look what it says here!" and I'd point to mine, "Well, look what it says here!" We enjoyed our morning fights.

She invited me to my first Seder, a big Seder where the conversations were conducted in half-a-dozen languages. Someone would say something in Russian, then someone else would respond in French, which would garner a retort in Romanian then, everyone would start speaking Yiddish. It just flowed. The sentiments were uttered in whichever language best expressed its intended tone and meaning. It was totally unconscious and completely inspiring.

Unfortunately, l'École des Beaux Arts was not. The school itself was freezing cold, with no heat, and I was used to Shanghai's stifling summers. I tried to draw wearing a bulky coat. I'd sit there with my big sketchpad, a little stool and attempt to draw from statuary. We were supposed to copy the old Greek and Roman statues in charcoal.

There was no instructor. Nobody cared what you did. Nobody even looked at it or talked to you. How was I supposed to learn anything about the mechanics?

I was disappointed with the school, and for the first time in my life, I was living without my family right on top of me in every moment. It was jarringly different. I spent great stretches of time without talking to anyone after an entire childhood spent with lots and lots of people in tiny spaces. All of a sudden, there were no people. There was no family. I missed Papa. I missed Mutti. I missed my sister, my friends, and all the noisy arguments. There was too much stillness.

My dinners with Charlie and his wife helped me immensely. Anytime Charlie was in town, (he traveled constantly), he'd invite me to eat with them. He spoke quite openly about the work he did with refugees. He told me about the Jewish communities all over the world. "In obscure corners, Jews can be found." I was always surprised he could move so freely from country to country, going back and forth as if it were nothing to cross war-torn borders. I was intensely curious about this ability of his, but I said nothing. His wife was a sweet lady, not Jewish and also from Philadelphia, quite reserved. She treated me like a son. They had no children of their own.

Since Charlie was not often in town, I had to make a major adjustment if I was going to outlast my loneliness. First, I ventured to a concert by myself. Then I went to an opera, then the beach, then a museum, and suddenly I realized I didn't need anyone around. I would be okay on my own. My French improved. I made new friends. I met girls, and the city of lights lit up. That's when I fell in love with Paris.

At Charlie's suggestion and with even more of his seemingly infinite help, I left l'École des Beaux Arts and transferred to Academie Julian where I liked the teachers, and it was nice and warm. It couldn't be cold! We sketched using naked models. Stunningly beautiful, Parisian models, naked right in front of us, and yet, if a pretty girl walked by in a tight red sweater, every painter would turn around and say, "Did you see her?"

Our models would pose in five-minute sessions, and we'd make quick impressions. Then the model would pose for fifteen minutes, and we'd sketch, then she'd return from her break and do one final thirty-minute pose. I loved working this way. I had to work so fast just to get the form, the movement of the body. I'd be happy with my drawing, and then one of the teachers would come over, draw right over top of it, fix all my problems, and then I could see...Aha! That's what it should look like.

I was studying realism, working from live models and still lifes. One of our instructors dumped a dead rabbit on a board. The odor burned your eyes, it was so rank. We squinted and attempted to paint around the searing pain in our nostrils. I held my breath and tried to breathe through my mouth. The other students ran out. They couldn't take the smell. I painted as long as I could, then I finally had to leave. Still, my painting of the dead, stinky rabbit won first prize.

It was my first experience with oil paint, though later, I would switch to acrylics. I was basically on my own because the studio system was informally structured. The teacher would come by once a week to critique my work, often destroying it, which can be quite liberating if you are serious about painting. In Cezanne, I discovered a new way of looking at nature. The complexity and underlying simplicity and the structure appealed to me. I was, after all, a tailor and a tailor's son. Then, there was Picasso. He broke all the rules, opening the window to endless possibilities. A breath of fresh air.

My fellow artists were almost entirely men, a few women, but the majority of my classmates were French and Jewish and American GIs on the GI Bill of Rights. The French and the Jews had survived the war by fighting, hiding or escaping. Some of the men had tattoos on their arms. Concentration-camp numbers. The Americans were war vets. Out of all of us, my life in the Shanghai ghetto had been the least traumatic. We lived our new lives in two languages;

English and French, though my letters back to Mutti were written in German. It would have been an affectation to send her letters in English, I wasn't trying to show off.

My skills as an artist improved so the Joint sent me to Marseilles to document a JDC refugee camp of North African Jews temporarily resettled in France before their permanent move to what would soon become Israel. They wanted me to make some drawings of the camp children and the environment. I drew things as I saw them in Marseilles. Just like I'd drawn exactly what I'd seen growing up in Vienna and in Shanghai, the soldiers and the broken-down beggars and the prostitutes. In Marseilles, I drew children with distended bellies covered in rags. I drew the misery and the poverty I saw. They weren't happy enough drawings for the JDC to use, but I had to be true to what I witnessed

Still, they paid me, which was a welcome influx of cash. I was living on one hundred dollars a month, eating in student cafeterias for forty cents a meal. Life as an artist in Paris I adored. Being broke all the time, not so much.

Charlie's advice had never steered me wrong, which is why over one of our dinners, I talked about my future. Would I be able to make a living as an artist? What should I do? In Shanghai, I never thought about my future, what my career should be, or how I would make a living. Our concerns were basic and primary: survival. Today, tomorrow, and maybe the day after tomorrow, our focus was on eating. I apprenticed as a tailor because Papa needed the help and I needed a trade. It was never meant to be my career. Career was a foreign word to my ears. I didn't know how to think so far ahead.

Charlie presented me with two options. I could go into advertising, or I could look at fashion. Advertising seemed like hot air, the promotion of someone else's creativity. At least in fashion, good, better, or different, something new was created. I'd grown up surrounded by tailors and fabric, needles, and thread. I liked the structure of building a coat or a suit. I knew that world.

Through Charlie's connections, I became a sketcher for couturier Alex Maguy, whose real name was Alex Glass, a Jew who'd been one of the few active members of the Resistance. After the war, he got his business back from the Germans, and though he wasn't one of the first names in fashion, like Dior or St. Laurent or Balenciaga, he claimed to be haute couture, and he had plenty of work for me to do.

I wasn't nervous at all my first day working for Mr. Maguy. I'd already worked as a sketcher for the most demanding designer on the face of the planet. Papa. All those years sketching men's suits in Shanghai, Papa had trained me well. After two wonderful years of getting to be a full-time artist, I was back in the schmatte business.

SISTER

I really missed Ilie. So did Mutti. When his letters would reach us, she'd read them to me, and I tried to imagine the wretched stink of the dead rabbit he drew, the sounds of the operas he heard, the laughter of his new friends. My life in Shanghai paled in comparison. All my friends were gone. Communists were threatening to occupy the city, and our money was useless. Monetary values changed hour by hour. A movie ticket skyrocketed to $10,000 Shanghai dollars. People carried bags of money instead of wallets. They just kept printing it.

Shanghai had always been corrupt, but now, it was completely out of control. Everything was greasing palms. The only way to do business was bribery. For enough money, you could buy a Chinese general and his army. You could take over a province, split the spoils, and walk away rich. There was a café, the Mars Café, where all those transactions took place. The black market was filled with army surplus. The soldiers drove their Jeeps into the ocean and sank them. There was nowhere to put them.

Papa still wouldn't leave. He was certain "the Communists had no issues with Jews," in the same way he'd been certain the "British would make mincemeat out of Hitler." The war was over, but my life hadn't changed. I didn't resent Ilie's leaving at all. I just added him to my list of tomorrows. Tomorrow, we would leave Shanghai. Tomorrow, we would go to America. Tomorrow, I would see Ilie again. Tomorrow, tomorrow, tomorrow.

To fill the loneliness of our emptier apartment, I got a pen pal from the United States. We were both barely teenagers, just turned thirteen. Our communications were facilitated by the JDC. He wrote me letters and sent me little care baskets. We wrote about our lives and compared to mine, his sounded wonderful. He didn't have a pool, but he had a real house, and his parents had a car. He told me that he "had to eat his broccoli because the kids in Europe didn't have any food." I imagined there were an awful lot of children in America suffering through their veggies for me. They could have them! My pen pal couldn't understand why I couldn't travel freely or leave China. He wrote a letter asking, "You have no choice?" and that phrase "no choice" really struck me. I couldn't articulate what it meant to have no choices to him because I'd never had any to begin with. I wasn't even sure I knew what the word "choice" meant.

Then one day, I came home from school, and I was sitting by the window looking out, daydreaming. I saw soldiers, different soldiers, real soldiers not like those ragamuffin Chinese soldiers with the straw hats and flip-flops. These soldiers were Chinese, but they were marching, and they had uniforms. Scary uniforms. Mutti yelled for me to start packing. The rest is a blur. We couldn't take any of the furniture. Mutti wanted to keep the hand-carved chest with ivory inlay. Impossible. I left Susie, my handless doll behind. We couldn't even take our clothes just whatever we could quickly grab, and we left. It was Vienna all over again. We left with nothing and ran to this enormous gray troop carrier called the *General Gordon*. My parents were relieved to leave, but were in a daze.

I asked Mutti, "Where are we going?"

Mutti said, "America."

For ten years, I had begged for America, and finally, we were going. As the ship pulled away, I just wanted it to hurry up, hurry up. The inches were not fast enough. I kept thinking, "Oh, please just keep going. I don't want to be pulled back! I hope nothing happens to the motor or the engine." I never wanted to touch ground in Shanghai ever again. Once again, we were on the last ship out. Last boat out of Vienna, because of Papa's stubbornness, and for the same reason, we were among the last people to leave Shanghai.

The boat was filled with God knows how many refugees and a handful of soldiers. There were no Chinese on the boat, only Germans or Russians or Indians or Poles or Austrians. Not necessarily all Jewish, but definitely all fleeing China. The men and the women were separated. Mutti was with me the whole time, but Papa had to sleep elsewhere. There were shared communal bathrooms and a mess hall I never got to see because I spent most of the three week journey sitting outside on the deck, wrapped in a blanket, drinking fizzy club soda, and eating crackers. I had a horrible case of seasickness. It didn't help that our beds were swinging hammocks. I was miserable.

The first port was Hawaii. People saw the ships, and they brought cookies and milk to the children. I don't remember the cookies, but I sure remember the milk because I'd never tasted real milk before. I'd had condensed milk or powdered milk mixed with water, but not fresh milk. It was cold and creamy and rich. Luxurious. It tasted like money. I'd been seasick for the entire three weeks it took to get to the United States, laying on my hammock, swinging back and forth, wanting to die, but you better believe I drank that milk and ate those cookies. People gave us M&Ms, and I'd never seen anything like them. They were amazing. They tasted like friendly ground, like the good life I hoped to have.

I asked Mutti, "This is not part of China, is it?"

Papa butted in, "Of course it's not part of China! It's Hawaii. It's a separate island. It's not really part of the mainland United States."

I had to be certain we had actually left. I asked again, "You're sure it's not China?"

Mutti insisted it was almost the United States, but not quite yet. "It's an island! It's lovely. It's beautiful. Don't you remember the movie?"

I didn't remember any movies about an island with palm trees, but I trusted America was close by.

From Hawaii, we went to San Francisco, and Mutti threw money at the Golden Gate Bridge for good luck. They made us wear identification tags, and I swore right then and there, I would never ever wear another. I felt like a refugee all over again. It was worse for us because we were stateless, and stateless was a notch below refugee. I mean, at least some people had a home country. We had no passports. We only had visas to be in the States as visitors, not to stay as residents. We stayed in a little hotel on Market Street near Chinatown in San Francisco. The minute I stepped onto the sidewalk, I realized I was surrounded by Chinese Americans. I thought I'd been tricked. I thought they had shipped me back to China. I thought the captain had made a U-turn in the ocean.

We didn't stay long in San Francisco. We traveled to New York by train, and when we got off at Penn Station, we were met at the station by Papa's sister. He hadn't seen her in forty years. I'd never met her, but I recognized her immediately. She looked just like him. They could have been twins. It was an emotional reunion. First, I was surprised to learn I had an auntie, and then, and this was the most shocking part, Papa hugged her, and she hugged him.

I had never seen Papa hug anyone including Mutti, his own wife. He had never hugged me! He didn't even hug Ilie goodbye when he left for Paris. Survival had been more important than cuddling. Affection had no place among us. Watching Papa hug his sister was like seeing an extraterrestrial land on Earth. I felt I had witnessed the impossible. The unnatural. It smacked against me like a teacher swatting a ruler to the hand. Fast, sharp, and leaving me breathless.

Fortunately, Papa had planned ahead. In Shanghai, whatever extra money he made, he always got it out of the country and sent it to my cousin in Washington Heights. Our cousin would save it for us, and if we never got out of Shanghai, it would be his. It was pure trust. There wasn't any written contract between them that proved Papa sent him money, but luckily, our cousin was an honorable man, and he saved it all for us. Papa didn't want to be a burden on my aunt, so he asked her, "What's the best building in the city?" We had a couple thousand dollars, not a lot. She told him "the Waldorf Astoria," which didn't mean a thing to me, but Papa rented a hotel room with a Pullman kitchen, and we settled into our new life.

I enrolled in school though when I tried to fill out a form with my address, I didn't know where I lived. I knew how to get back to my building by bus, but I didn't know the exact address. Eyebrows rose. I didn't know my address? I came back the next day and wrote the Waldorf Astoria with the exact address and the number of the room. The kids ridiculed me. They thought I was too embarrassed to say where I lived. I didn't even know I was staying in a fancy hotel.

I made my first American friend, Sandra, and I got very close to her. The months passed quickly until one day, I came home from school ready to go out and play with Sandra when Mutti announced, "We're leaving."

I argued, "I have to do my homework."

Mutti was already packing. "Never mind the homework."

I was devastated. "Where are we going?"

Mutti answered me abruptly. "Canada."

I couldn't understand why we had to leave again. "Is that in the United States?"

Mutti just shook her head. "No. Close."

I had no say in the matter. I cried my eyes out. I had to tell Sandra I was leaving. She was wearing pigtails and crying. I yelled at Mutti, "I'll never have another friend again!"

It didn't matter what I said, off we went to Canada. From that moment on, I decided there would be no more tearful goodbyes. Every goodbye felt final, and I had no control over my leaving or other people leaving me. It was better just to stay detached. No more friends for me.

We moved to Montreal. At the border, the immigration official kept insisting we were moving to Canada as immigrants, but Mutti kept insisting right back we were, "Only visitors! Only visitors!" They stamped our visas with "visitors," and I should have paid more attention to that. I should have known we would move again.

We lived on St. Lawrence Boulevard. There was an older woman who lived by herself in an apartment, and she rented two bedrooms to us. My parents took one room, and I had the other though my room was more of a hallway. I couldn't lock myself in. There was nothing to lock. We shared the kitchen with the older woman and a communal bathroom. We managed. After nearly ten years in Shanghai, Montreal wasn't difficult. It was clean and quiet, and there were no dead bodies in the streets or bugs crawling over my bed at night. Life had improved considerably even if it wasn't America.

Papa found work as a tailor, and I enrolled in Catholic school. I had to wear a navy tunic with a white blouse that Mutti hand washed at the end of each week. They offered advanced courses. I took trigonometry at thirteen. I wasn't a triple-A student, but I was a B-plus. I didn't like sports or climbing the ropes or the monkey bars. I faked illnesses because I was afraid. China had turned me into a frightened person, and the fearful part of me was always in control. Anything I hadn't experienced before was very uncomfortable to me. Ultimately, I had no choice. I had to climb those stupid monkey bars.

The school was cliquish because my classmates had grown up together. I was the refugee, shown up out of nowhere. I didn't like the teachers. They were very strict. I did well in school because I had nothing else to do except go home and do homework. My saving grace, once again, was the movies. I lucked out. There was a movie house right underneath our apartment. Unfortunately, in Canada, I had to be sixteen to see a movie unescorted, and they were strict about it. It wasn't like China where I could sneak in unnoticed. I tried lying about my age, but I was kicked out. I put on lipstick and tried again. That didn't work, either. My parents had to chaperone, and they couldn't just drop me off. They had to sit through the film. Problem was my parents weren't moviegoers; they didn't care for them. So I turned myself into the apartment's official dishwasher, though there were plenty of nights when all the dishes in the world would not help my cause. It never crossed my mind that Papa didn't have the money to spend on such frivolous nonessentials. I just felt he was mean and didn't want me to go for some obscure parent reason that made sense only to parents.

The only time Papa would acquiesce to my begging and pleading was if the cinema was showing a Western. Fortunately, all they ever showed in Canada were cowboy films and Roy Rogers on his horse. I wasn't a fan of Westerns, but Papa loved them, and he'd go willingly if there were guns and cowboys. I learned not to complain. As long as it moved and was on the screen, I was happy. Even though the Canadian theaters were tiny. In Shanghai, the houses might have been filthy, but they were grand. They seated eight hundred people at a show. It was a whole experience to sit among hundreds of people watching and reacting to a film. I liked feeling swallowed up by the experience. Canadian theaters were tiny in comparison. I longed for the spectacle, the drama of the biggest screens. In that one instance, I missed Shanghai, but I learned to settle for the smaller versions of my favorite stars. Plus, our landlady had a record player and a few records including the soundtrack from the Tarzan movie. She let me listen to it repeatedly. I would try to remember the scenes from the movie. Every once in a while, I heard him screaming, and I just yearned for Tarzan to come and get me! I would have swung from tree to tree happily in his arms.

Canada turned out to be a happier move than I expected. I made

friends, enjoyed my daily routine, and was reasonably happy counting down the days until I turned sixteen so I could go see movies on
my own. Then, Ilic came to join us in Canada. I hadn't seen him in
years. When he walked through the door, I almost didn't recognize
him. He was so thin, almost like a skeleton. I was thrilled to see him.
My parents were happy, too, but I could tell that Ilie missed Paris.
He didn't want to be in Canada. He missed his Parisian life and no
wonder. After strolling by the Seine, he must have been bored out
of his mind with us.

I didn't realize Ilie's arrival meant we were moving again. Mutti
started packing. She announced, "We're finally going to the United
States permanently!"

I said, "Who wants to go there now? I'm perfectly happy here!"

I'd forgotten about Mutti's insistence we were "only visitors" at
the border. I'd learned French and gotten comfortable. I'd promised
myself I wouldn't get attached to friends, but I'd done it again, set
myself up for more heartbreak. I didn't want to move anymore. My
whole life had been one goodbye after another to everything and
everybody. Goodbye was my only constant. We were nomads, still
refugees, and I absolutely refused to believe America would be my
permanent home. It had been taken from me once before. There was
no way I was getting tricked into hoping again. I refused to pack my
things. Mutti could pack them if she wanted, but I wasn't helping.

BROTHER

In 1948, I was in Paris, loving life when Charlie explained to me
that the United States and Soviet Union were officially recogniz-
ing the state of Israel and the American Congress was going to pass
the Displaced Persons Act authorizing 200,000 displaced people to
enter the United States. Up until the act passed, the quota system was
intact. The world was struggling to recover from the war, and hun-

dreds of thousands of Jews were wasting away in refugee camps, still trying to reunite with their families and take permanent residence somewhere, anywhere. All of that was about to change.

The Displaced Persons Act meant I could move to America and become a United States citizen. Charlie told me, "There is a window of opportunity. I suggest you avail yourself of it. Get to Canada with your parents." My family was already in Montreal where Mutti had had the good sense to insist they be classified as visitors. Had she allowed the border guards to classify them as immigrants, they would not have been eligible for the DPA. They would be moving back to New York within three months, and if I wanted citizenship, I needed to join them. It was my best shot. I had to act.

Charlie arranged for a visitor's visa to Canada and my passage. The journey was uneventful. I was a pro at massive life upheavals via steamship. I met Papa in Quebec and was pleased to see he looked exactly as I remembered him. Round and stout. From there, we took the train to Montreal. Mutti had not changed at all, but Dorit had grown taller. Nothing else had changed. After two years in Paris, Montreal was a letdown. I resigned myself to the boredom and filled it with painting and drawing since three months wasn't enough to put down real roots, get a job, or build a new life.

P*ART IV*

NEW YORK, HOUSTON, NEW JERSEY, SAN FRANCISCO

BROTHER

We were finally allowed into America as immigrants applying for permanent residency and citizenship. The four of us moved into a railroad apartment on West Ninety-fourth Street, and after two years on my own, I worried it might cramp my freedom to move back in with my parents and my sister. It didn't. I had my own room, and I came and went as I pleased. I didn't see my family much. A distance had grown between my father and me. We'd been very close in Shanghai, discussing politics and history and the war, but Paris had been the first tiny loose thread that loosened the hem. New York opened the entire seam. The closeness we had once shared had disappeared. The generation gap became a chasm. I only came home to sleep.

Industrious as ever, Papa quickly found a job, but this time, he took work as a fitter. It was a major step down. His reputation in

Vienna and Shanghai meant nothing in New York. He was used to being respected, but now, he was merely a number. Plus, he had never really learned English. His generation, the older generation, were always secretly hoping to return to Vienna from Shanghai. Austria was their home, their history, and their entire life. They remembered the good times and were protective of their native tongues. Even in Shanghai, Papa inhabited a circle of men who spoke only Yiddish, Romanian, German, or Russian. On that one rare instance when he needed to speak with the Japanese commander, he used a translator: me. The transaction had taken place in broken English, which I then translated into German. It was the only time Papa was forced to deal with the English language for his livelihood.

But now in New York, he had no choice about it. Taking the job as a fitter was a harsh blow to his ego as well as his wallet. Mutti went back to work, taking a job in a millinery to help make ends meet. Her English was much better than his. She'd spent all those mornings navigating the Chinese markets where the language of bartering was pidgin English with a British accent.

As for me, I was having a tough time making a go of it. I could not find a job as a designer or sketcher despite the fact I'd been interviewing for eight months. Everyone wanted American experience, but how was I supposed to get American experience if I couldn't land an American job? Cold-calling was useless. If I did get in the door, I was treated terribly. I saw the assistant of an assistant, or they left me waiting for hours. One of the men very condescendingly flipped through my book, pinched my cheek, and told me, "It's not for us, kiddo." Years later, his son would try to become a partner in my business.

I was frustrated and broke, but Papa kept encouraging and financially supporting me, as well. He did not want me to work as a tailor. He wanted me to wait for the right opportunity. "You have to start in couture. If you start in couture, you can always work cheap. If you start cheap, you can never work in couture." My cousins pressured me to take any job at all. "You're a tailor! Take a job as a tailor! What's this with designing?" But Papa would not hear a word of it. "Never! He will never be a tailor!" Papa and I, we were snobs the same way. We both wanted to see me at a top house.

I decided to get tricky about it. I honed my French accent and called a designer named Philip Mangone. He'd been one of the passengers on the Hindenburg when it crashed. He'd saved lives, but was badly burned during the rescue. His face was marked with skin grafts. He had a very successful business specializing in suits. He worked mostly in wool. I got his secretary. I told her, "I've just flown in from Paris, and I'd like an appointment with Monsieur Mangone." I didn't mention I was looking for a job. It worked. The secretary scheduled an appointment for me with Mr. Mangone personally. He had a leonine appearance with big white hair and broad shoulders. He liked my sketches, so he hired me. It took almost an entire year to find my first job, but I was finally where I wanted to be.

The Mangone manufacturing operations were quite large. Our main offices were located on Seventh Avenue with the showrooms and a blouse factory on site. But the operation was so large, not all the suits could be made there. We had four smaller plants in the Garment District. I became the sketcher for Mr. Mangone's designer, a former model and his ex-wife. She was quite old and crotchety. She'd hand me scribbles. "Make me this and this." I had no idea what she wanted, so I made my own sketches instead, though I never got or took credit for those designs.

I watched Mr. Mangone carefully. He ran the entire business by himself. A customer would come in. The model would show the suit, and the customer would ask the price. Mr. Mangone would make up a price based on the appearance of the customer, and somehow, he managed to remember exactly what he charged each person. He was notoriously cheap. I'd ask for a raise, and he'd say, "We lost money this season." He'd expected to make two million dollars and instead he only made a million seven. He lost money.

I learned to develop a very thick skin. No raise? Okay, so no raise. Hate the sketch? Okay, tear it up and make another one. I learned to keep my ego out of design and to not take fashion seriously. Like Woody Allen said about showing up, I learned to just do the job and stick with it. I had talent, and I knew eventually, I would succeed. Designing clothes wasn't brain surgery. I'd survived Hitler in Vienna and the ghetto in Shanghai. I could survive the fashion industry in New York. No problem.

SISTER

The minute we made it back to New York, I was certain our lives would become perfect, but I was wrong. Papa had spent all the money he saved in Shanghai during our four months at the Waldorf Astoria. While we were in Canada, I knew we were in trouble when there was nothing but hard-boiled eggs and matzo crackers to eat. I kept my mouth shut, as did my parents, and we never owned up to it. In China, everyone was poor. In Canada, we could get by, but that was not the case in America. In America, it was very clear that we were poor.

Papa refused to ask our relatives for help. He'd rather starve and give his last dime to a beggar on the street. His pride was all he had. America was a total disappointment to him and to me. I realized, slowly, the pool wasn't going to happen, there would be no house. After all those years dreaming of a magnificent land of wealth and luxury, America wasn't anything like the movies.

Once again, we were powerless. Money was power, and we had none. Having not had it as a child, I felt my family was stepped on, degraded. America made the class difference all the more profound. In China, we were all refugees. We were all displaced persons. We were as low as you could get. It became very clear, once we got to New York, unless you were very wealthy, no one was going to respect you.

People looked down on you. Nobody said it directly to me, but I got the general gist. I was the poor relative.

I saw my friends going off to vacations in the summer, and my parents couldn't afford to send me anywhere. One of my friends invited me to join them, but I wouldn't go because I didn't want to be the person who showed up in a lavish home and was so impressed. I didn't want to be the deprived kid. Even at my cousin's house, I wouldn't sit by their pool. I just refused. I didn't want to feel like a charity case. Plus, I didn't know how to swim. With my childhood adoration of Esther Williams and pools, you'd think I would have taken to water like a fish, but quite the opposite was true. I was deathly afraid of water, of oceans and pools. Mutti used to take me to the beach. I dragged along behind. She told me, "If you don't go into the water and swim, I'm leaving. I'm never coming back to the beach." I was too afraid to go in. Finally, she took me to the public pool and made me get in. I pretended I was swimming and just walked back and forth, swaying my arms, but keeping my feet on the bottom of the pool until the water hit my neck. Of course, Mutti could see my legs weren't behind me. I pushed myself to really pretend, and I got into the deeper water without realizing it. I couldn't walk anymore. It terrified me, but I learned to swim fast.

Financially, we were also treading water, but as far as my education was concerned, the teachers weren't sure if I was sinking or swimming. In math, I was so far ahead, I'd already taken trigonometry, but I was painfully shy. I never raised my hand, and if they called on me, I felt like I would die. I was no Esther Williams. I was a fish out of water. Because the teachers had no way to determine my skills, they decided to give me an IQ test.

I had x amount of time to take the test. The math part was not a big deal, but the reading part was in English. My English was not great. In Canada, I went to a French school, and in China, I went to a British school, but my native language was German. I didn't understand half the questions, so I thought, "I'll just leave it blank." I left probably 75 percent of those circles empty. I scored a 96. I thought, "96 out of 100 is pretty good!" In our class, everything was scaled to 100. Once I realized the scale went over 100, I kept my score to myself. I had essentially failed.

From that point on, I assumed I was stupid. It never occurred to me to explain I didn't understand the questions. It never occurred to me to ask to take it again. None of my teachers could understand how I could do so well in math and have a photographic memory with my score being so low. I got by strictly with memorization. I could memorize a page, visualize the side of the book it was on, even where I had read the book and what was next to me. Comprehension was another matter entirely. God forbid somebody asked me what I felt or thought. I wouldn't have been able to speak.

I was pretending all the time. I wanted to lose my accent so nobody could tell where I was from. I wanted to be seen as American, but trying to downplay my accent made it a different kind of accent, even stronger. I would forget to pay attention, and it would leak out. I tried to think of every word and what it should sound like before I opened my mouth to speak. It was exhausting. I tried very hard to say "class" the way Americans did instead of a British-sounding "clahss," but I always slipped and embarrassed myself. My accent became an amalgamation from a land unrecognizable, part Viennese, part Chinese, part British, part American, part Hollywood movie star. Certain words might reveal me, but on the whole, my accent just kept people guessing, which is exactly how I liked it.

Papa still made all my clothes, and this time, there were no parents lining up for their own version of an army-blanket coat. My clothes were modest to the point of being matronly. Papa was so overprotective, he rode the subways with me, wouldn't allow me to wear lipstick, and he wanted me covered from head to toe. Most of my dates used to say, "Why don't you ever wear something a little sexier?" But Papa always thought I showed too much skin. I learned to alter the garments, making removable pieces to cover my neck and chest that could secretly be taken off once out of his sight. Papa never actually taught me to sew. I watched him, then made my own designs, which, of course, he would supervise. Unsolicited. He was a stickler for seams and lining. He believed the inside had to look as good as the outside. That meant I had to really double seam the pieces and do very fine hems by hand. He wouldn't let me use a machine. The work was delicate. I had to put a stitch, fold it, and then go underneath and make another and go underneath so the stitches would not show.

I did my best to hide my "sexy" alterations from him, and the minute I got in my friend's car, I took the altered pieces off my dress and put my lipstick on. On the way home, I'd redress and wipe off the lipstick. Of course, one night, I was running half an hour late and missed my curfew of 10 p.m. I rushed so I forgot to wipe the red off my lips. Papa yelled, "Tramp!" and grounded me for a week.

I was ping-ponging between my parents' mixed messages. Papa wanted to keep me a little girl while Mutti wanted me to become a model or a movie star. I was tall and full of freckles, and Mutti thought my look was marketable. We went to a couple of agencies for go-sees. I wore a mint-green silk dress with a tiny waist and a high neck. They asked us for a glossy, which I didn't have, and they looked me up and down, made me turn around to the left, turn around to the right. One of them said, "Great eyes—too skinny." One of them said, "Too tall." One of them said, "Too many freckles." When they asked me to smile, I couldn't smile on demand.

Mutti decided I needed a professional picture. We went to Weitzman Photographers, and they posed me, looking over my left shoulder. They superimposed the image onto a huge slab of marble and kept it in their window. A casting director saw it and wanted to cast me in a shampoo commercial. Papa vetoed that option immediately. Then I snuck off to enter a beauty contest in New Jersey. I bought a red two-piece bathing suit—it wasn't a skimpy bikini, but it was a two-piece—and I entered the contest. I paraded up and down before I saw Papa in the audience. He marched over and dragged me off the stage. Just like he'd ended Mutti's chance of becoming Miss Austria, Papa ended my pageant dreams with a declaration. There would be no more pageants. End of discussion.

Mutti then decided I should become a singer. She hired a vocal coach I totally disliked because before I could sing a note, she wanted me to learn how to play the piano. Mutti felt we could skip the lessons and go straight to radio instead. She dragged me to a radio station where they put me in a booth. I was so naive. I really believed nobody could hear me. I sang my heart out, "Blue mooooooooooon. I saw you standing aloooooooooone." When I came out, Mutti said, "That was pretty good!" I was mortified. I would never go back. I was just too shy to shine.

Mutti tried to turn me into the woman, the beauty queen, the Miss Austria she wanted to be, she never got to be because of her country and her husband and the circumstances of her life. Maybe that's why she tried to live through me in those days. She wanted desperately for me to shine, and I played along because it felt like Hollywood. It felt like a movie and being a movie star, had to be the best life anyone could live. Movie stars had servants and pools and money, and they certainly didn't eat hard-boiled eggs for breakfast, lunch, and dinner.

But to be a movie star, you couldn't be shy. You couldn't refuse to sing, and you certainly had to be able to smile on demand. You couldn't walk around fearful of life. You couldn't be invisible. All the things I'd been trained to be. I was still the little girl peeking out from behind the curtain, though I wanted desperately to be noticed. I wished I had Papa's bravado and Ilie's talents, then I could have smiled for the cameras, I could have belted out a song. I didn't have either. I was my mother's daughter, a woman in a culture and an age when women became wives and that was enough. It was supposed to be enough.

BROTHER

Having moved to New York, I was now eligible for citizenship. I was given a booklet to study, and so I prepared for my test diligently. My friends walked me downtown to the Manhattan courthouse. I was supposed to go before a judge and answer questions such as, "How many senators does a state have?" "Who was the first president?" "Who was the second president?" but right before I got called into the courtroom, my friend punched me and said, "They're going to ask you what were Custer's last words?" I shrugged my shoulders, "I don't know what he said." My friend laughed and said, "Where did all those fucking Indians come from?" I had a tough time keeping a straight face from that point on, but I answered the questions correctly and was allowed to swear in with a big group.

We gathered in the United States District Court on Pearl Street in Manhattan, raised our right hands, and promised to "absolutely and entirely renounce and abjure all allegiance and fidelity to any foreign prince, potentate, state, or sovereignty of whom or which I have heretofore been a subject or citizen."[1] It was an easy promise to make seeing I'd never considered myself loyal to any land. China certainly wasn't home and just the thought of Vienna brought my blood to a boil. Before that moment, no land had wanted me, had ever laid claim to my person. For the first time in my life, I was a citizen, fully recognized and honored. I got my first legitimate passport. It said American. Suddenly, I was no longer stateless. I was an American. I had almost resigned myself to being stateless. I was so used to it. I knew no other way. I never imagined it would feel so great to become a citizen. It was an amazing feeling.

---

1 *Oath of Allegiance for Naturalized Citizens,* Citizenship and Immigration Services, U.S. Department of Homeland Security, http://www.uscis.gov/portal/site/uscis

Our family leaving Vienna. On board SS Conte Biancamane, *1939*

ABOVE: *Ilie's sketch of the view from our window on Chusan Road in Shanghai, 1945. This is the tiny space our family of four shared.*

BELOW: *This photo is the same view from the same room taken in 1987 when Ilie accompanied Deborah's family on a return trip to Shanghai.*

ABOVE: *Ilie's sketch of the "apartment" - 1-1/4 rooms, including Dad's workplace (he was a tailor, hence the mannequin in the corner), living room, bedroom, and kitchen; outdoor bathroom and toilet were communal.*
RIGHT: *Ilie's drawing of the stove Mutti cooked on during the war. It was sort of a Chinese version of a hibachi.*

LEFT: *Deborah on the left, with friends Peter, in the middle, and Judy on the right. Photo was taken in Shanghai by a Japanese photographer who was looking for well-dressed children for a propaganda shot. Deborah was attending a reunion meeting with Judy when they found the original photo hanging on the wall! The girls had stayed in touch for years and Judy actually introduced Deborah to her husband, Ed.*

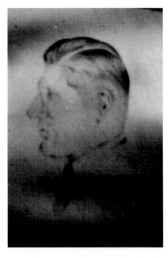

Our family in Shanghai, 1946. Our mother and father, Helen and Moritz with Ilie behind and Deborah in front.

This drawing of Charles Jordan by Ilie was the sketch that was responsible for Ilie going to Paris.

Taken in front of our school in 1949, the day before Ilie left Shanghai. The family didn't know if they would ever see each other again.

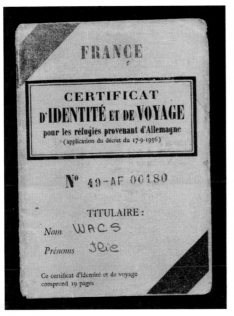

Various travel documents, including a passport Ilie used to travel to Paris

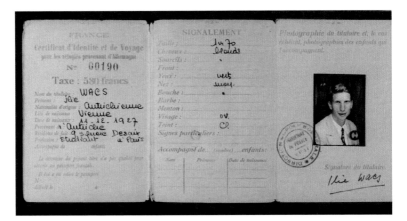

LEFT: *Charles Jordan and Ilie in Paris, 1949*

BELOW: *Ilie, Charles Jordan and a friend in Paris*

Another view of Chusan Road taken in 1987 on Deborah's and Ilie's return to Shanghai.

This photo of a memorial was taken in Hongkou, also in 1987. The inscription reads " From 1937 to 1941, thousands of Jews came to Shanghai fleeing from Nazi persecution. Japanese authorities regarded them as "stateless refugees" and set up this designated area to restrict their residence and business…."

Deborah and husband hosted a lunch for Prime Minister Yitzhak Rabin in early 1980. It was held at the Fairmont Hotel in San Francisco

As Deputy Chief of Protocol in San Francisco in 1986, Deborah met President Bill Clinton on his arrival at the airport. He took part in a conference with other world leaders held to celebrate the 50th anniversary of the signing of the United Nations charter.

The Strobin family in 1997. Son Mitchell in front, on the left is husband, Edward and son Mark in the back. This was the last photo taken of the complete family.

OPPOSITE, TOP: *Maris, Ilie, Darin and Sylvia: this photo appeared in the New York Times in June, 1969 along with a feature article about Ilie.*

OPPOSITE, BOTTOM: *Ilie, Sylvia, daughters Darin and Maris with Mutti in between them in 1968.*

RIGHT: *Ilie with his wife, Sylvia, in 1960*

BELOW: *Ilie with his companion, Susan, in 1990.*

Exit Visa II, 2000, mixed media on canvas, 40 x 64 inches

This series of works is based on personal experiences in pre-World War II Vienna, Austria, involving the documentation required by the Austrian/German government for Jews. The work derives its imagery from stamps, seals, passports, script, fragments of sentences and various symbols of authority.

A person was defined by official notarized description and without these papers one did not exist. It was the beginning of what was to follow.

Ilie Wacs

LEFT: *Invitation to Ilie's show (entitled "The Vienna Papers, 1938") held at the Pamela Williams Gallery in Amagansett, NY in the summer of 2004.*

BELOW: *Ilie at the Pamela Williams Gallery in 2004. Photo by Charles Traub.*

Ilie Wacs

The Vienna Papers, 1938

July 29 - August 14

Opening Reception: Saturday, July 29, 5 - 7 P.M.

PAMELA WILLIAMS GALLERY LTD.
167 Main Street, Amagansett, NY 631.267.7817 www.pamelawilliamsgallery.com
Friday through Monday, 11 - 6

"Collage"

"Color of Eyes"

"Exit Visa II"

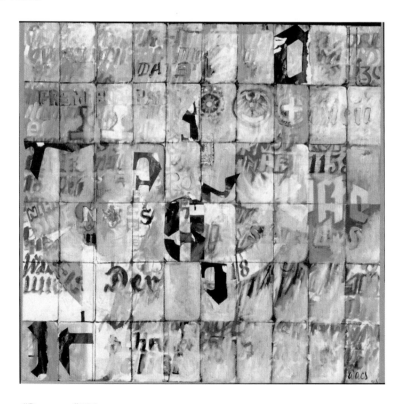

"Document"#30

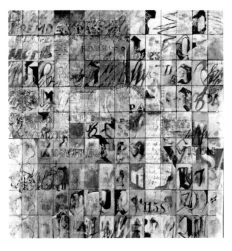

"Fremden Pass - Stateless"

"Passport"

"Falling Man"

"Silkprint"

"Stateless"

SISTER

Papa did not like any of the young men I was dating. I was close with Papa, and I wanted his approval, but none of my dates met his impossible standards. The boys had to come upstairs to meet him and get me, that was a requirement and the right thing to do, but once they were in the front door, they never stood a chance. Papa hated them all. He threw a few out because he didn't like their clothes! One date made the mistake of crossing his foot over his knee revealing a worn sole. Papa said to him, "Why don't you fix the hole in your shoe?" The guy quickly put his foot down. Papa kept sitting and staring at him. It was horribly awkward, I finally said, "I think we'd better go." Papa just got up. "So when are you bringing her back?" Oh, he brought me back all right. He couldn't wait to end our evening. That guy didn't ask for a second date.

Everybody was still an idiot in Papa's eyes no matter that New York stripped him of his power, his status, and his reputation. No matter he could no longer make a living doing what he loved or speak the language as well as his children or his wife. He still referred to most of my dates as fools. "That fool's on the phone," or "That idiot, what's-his-name, is at the door." If he said, "fool" he meant the nephew of Einstein who had piercing blue eyes and kept tugging at my clothes trying to take off my top. If Papa said "idiot," I knew it was John.

John was a Marine. An extremely sexy, good-looking, tall Marine. I loved that he was taller than me. I was tired of dating shorter men. I had to wear flats and hunch over on all of my dates. Ilie said to me, "Stand up straight. Let the guy worry about reaching you." John was extremely wealthy and lived on Park Avenue with his family. He called me Debbie. He preferred the nickname to Doris or Dorit, so I became Debbie to everyone except Papa who refused to use my new name. Papa absolutely hated John. Both my parents took an immediate dislike to him because his mother had been married five times. They felt it didn't bode well for our future, but I didn't care. I thought it unfair to judge him by his mother's actions. I just wanted to be with him. He was the sexiest guy.

John gave me a ring, a gold band with prongs holding a big South Sea pearl and little tiny diamonds encircling it. It was a perfect pearl, his grandmother's ring, but when I saw it, I was a bit let down. I was hoping for a diamond. Then he gave me his dog tags and a watch and with those three items in my possession, we were engaged to marry. I could not wear the ring in front of my parents. Hell would have had to freeze over for my parents to let us marry. Papa would have killed him first. I did, however, wear the watch, and I kept the dog tags on my dresser where I could see them, think of John, and dream about our future together.

That future was not meant to be. John came to pick me up, and I was still half-dressed in the bathroom getting ready. Papa rushed into my bedroom and grabbed the dog tags and the watch off my dresser. He tied them in a kerchief with a knot and handed them back to John. He threw him out of our house, told him never to come back, and slammed the door right in his face. I heard the commotion and came out.

Papa said to me, "You're staying home."

I said, "Wasn't that him?"

Papa folded his arm. "Yes it was him, and he's not coming back."

Ilie saw the whole scene. I yelled to Ilie, "I hate him, I hate him."

There was nothing he could do. I begged Mutti to help, but she wouldn't stand up to Papa. I was hysterical. I cursed Papa. Mutti wouldn't let me near a phone. I slammed the door to my room. I screamed and cried, "How can you do this? He's the love of my life!" My only consolation was my pearl engagement ring. Papa hadn't found it. I'd hidden it well. It was still mine.

Papa and Ilie knew John had cheated on me, but they didn't tell me, so I had no idea why Papa had been so cruel. It seemed so unfair. There was that word again. I began sneaking out to meet John. I'd tell my parents I was meeting girlfriend, who had strict instructions to cover for me, then John would pick me up and drop me off a couple of blocks away. We continued to date secretly for a year.

I would have married him had he not stood me up one too many times. There was a dance, and I bought a special gown for the occasion. It was sexier than my usual modest dresses with a lower neckline. John didn't show. I was just devastated. Ilie knew what happened and called one of his friends who still had a tux from a recent wedding and asked him to escort me. It was either go with Ilie's buddy or not go at all. I went, but I didn't want to dance. I just wanted to go home. I was dumped and heartbroken.

Then I got hard proof John was cheating. A friend of mine who happened to live in the building told me a story about a handsome Marine she met in the elevator. He had asked her for a date. I didn't tell her who he was. I called him and confronted him, and he admitted he cheated. He told me, "Since it's so clear you're untouchable, I'm still a man. I get it elsewhere out of respect for you." I was so naive and sheltered, I was actually touched by the sentiment. I actually considered taking him back.

Then a friend of mine, Judy, called to say she was engaged. "I want you to come to my engagement party. I even have a date for you." I didn't believe in blind dates, but I was fed up with John. She said, "What have you got to lose? He's got a new car." His name was Ed, and he was the cousin of Judy's fiancé. He didn't have a date either, so he essentially got assigned to me.

Ed called, and he sounded angry. "I'm supposed to pick you up."

I was taken aback by his straightforward demeanor. The conversation just got worse. He asked, "What do you look like?"

So I told him. "I'm tall and thin, have red hair, and I've got freckles."

When I heard him murmur "shit," I asked him, "What do you look like?"

He had the nerve to say, "I'm tall, dark, and handsome."

A few days later, he knocked on my door. I was so nervous I wouldn't come out of my room. I asked Mutti, "First of all, how tall is he? Should I wear a heel, a ballerina flat, go out barefoot, hunch over?"

Mutti said, "How do I know? He just walked in and sat."

I said, "Can't you figure it out?"

Mutti said, "Wear flats already, but you've got to come out, you can't not come out."

I ran out like lightning all the way past Ed and my parents into the kitchen. I was trying to catch a glimpse of him! I stayed in the kitchen because all I had seen was a blur of dark hair. Mutti came into the kitchen. "Why are you hiding in here?"

"I'm trying to figure out what he looked like."

She said "Either come out, or we're sending him home. It doesn't make sense. You can't stay in the kitchen. You'll make a foolish impression."

I wouldn't budge. I asked Mutti "Is he wearing a hat?"

Mutti said, "Why would he wear a hat?"

I said, "If he wore a hat, I'm not going out." I had this thing about men with hats. I worried they were trying to hide their baldness.

Mutti yelled, "Just come out!"

I reluctantly came out. I was nineteen years old and shy. I was dying on that walk from the kitchen to the living room. Then I saw him and damn it, he was just as good looking as he said he was. Tall, dark, and handsome. And apparently, I'd made quite the impression on him, as well. Seems when I'd zoomed past, Ed determined he was going to marry me. He told his friend later on, "The minute that blur ran by, I knew then and there. This was it."

We drove to his cousin's party. On the way over, we chatted, and Ed asked, "Why are you sitting so close to the door? You might fall out."

I said, "No, it's locked."

I was sitting as far away from Ed as possible. My shyness could be debilitating at times. When we got to the party, we danced, and I was trying to lead. Ed stopped right in the middle of the dance floor and said, "Okay. Let's make a decision. I lead or you lead, we can't both lead." I was taken aback and had to remind myself not to lead. We danced all night.

When he took me home, my mind raced. I worried the elevator might not work. I worried that I would have to walk up twelve flights of stairs. I worried Ed might not walk me to the door, but instead just let me out of the car to fend for myself. Enough with the worry. I decided to move a little bit closer to him. It was dumb to lean against the door even if I didn't want to appear aggressive. My hair was pulled back into a ponytail with a string of pearls. I didn't like the rubber bands, and I wouldn't wear a bow. Mutti had outbowed me to death in China, but every time I turned my head, I felt my ponytail pulling against the seat of the car. I loosened my hair and saw Ed do a double take. That's when I knew I had him.

He double-parked and insisted on walking me to my door. I said, "Well, have a good night." I knew Papa was on the other side of my door. Ed didn't budge. He asked for another date. I said I was busy.

He said, "Okay, what about the week after?"

I said, "I don't think I can make it then, either."

Ed tried again. "Okay . . . what about during the week?"

I said, "Oh, during the week, I really can't make it."

So he said, "What about the third week?" and at that point, he looked cross.

I said, "I don't know."

He sat down on the floor outside my door, blocking it.

I was confused. "Do you want to come in or something?"

He said, "I won't let you pass until you tell me exactly what day you're available. You can't be so tied up you don't have a day." He would not budge until I agreed to a date.

The minute I walked in the door, Mutti asked, "Well? Was he taller than you?" I said, "I probably could have worn a heel."

He called every single day until our next date. Every time he called, I hoped it was John. It never was. Mutti was crazy about Ed. Whenever he called, she was delighted. Papa even liked him. Ed was very straightforward and polite. He didn't feel threatened by Papa. He would sit and wait for me with confidence. Other boys cringed knowing Papa was examining them. They got anxious and kept looking at their watch. Ed didn't. He just sat there relaxed, took off his coat. Even Judy, who introduced us, didn't understand my hesitation. "Oh my God. He's so much better looking than John, what are you talking about?" I was still hung up on John. I had to force myself to reverse the feelings, to transfer them over to Ed.

I didn't think I would marry Ed. He was good to me, he was handsome, and he had a new car plus his parents were wealthy. There was nothing bad about him, but I wasn't in love. As the weeks passed and he persisted, I slowly told myself, "Hey, this is as good as it gets." I was nineteen, and all my friends were engaged or married. Here was someone who fell in love with me and couldn't stop chasing me. I gave him such little encouragement. Maybe that's what drove Ed crazy. Ed was used to women who fawned over him. He was handsome and a pilot. His family had money. He was a catch.

He was such a catch that he was already engaged to a senator's daughter. She was supposed to have been his date for the engagement party, but she couldn't attend. That was a party she shouldn't have missed. The week after our first date, he broke off with her. His mother was devastated. She had a son engaged to a senator's daughter, how impressive, and all of a sudden, here comes a redheaded refugee!

Even after Ed and I became exclusive, his mother kept a photo of the senator's daughter displayed in their living room. She was a very pretty, dark-haired young woman with a big black Doberman. I saw her picture and thought maybe she was a cousin. His mother had no problem telling me, "Oh, that was Ed's fiancé." I didn't hear the word "was" I just heard the word fiancé. It took a while for me to ask him about her.

"Ed, were you ever engaged?"

He said, "You knew I was. You saw her picture there."

I couldn't pull anything with Ed. He was so straightforward. I asked, "Why is it still there?"

He said, "Ask my mother. It's not in my room."

His parents disliked me on sight. They thought I was Irish. They spoke Hebrew not realizing I understood. His mother said, "My God, look at her there. He could have gotten someone to look a lot better in his own religion." I stood there smiling. His mother didn't like that I was poor. I was a refugee, a greenhorn, a newcomer. I hadn't been born in America, not that his parents were, either, but they'd be in the States longer and were snobs, very reactionary people. Bigoted. Had I been a wealthy refugee, his mother wouldn't have minded. She told him, "If you love someone, why not love a rich someone?"

In China, I never felt like a refugee. It was a word for other people. It did not attach itself to me until my soon-to-be mother-in-law placed it on my shoulders. She began referring to me as "the refugee" in conversation. Had I been braver, I would have said something, but I had learned from Mutti to stay quiet and keep my pain to myself. Plus, Ed was nothing like his mother. He could have cared less about her opinion of me. He was determined we would marry, and when Ed decided he wanted something, he got it.

On Valentine's Day, Ed gave me a wristwatch, and a month later, he called from the air-force base in Texas where he was stationed to tell me he'd be flying back to New York the week of April 13, and we were getting married. I said, "What?" He said, "We are getting married." It took me completely by surprise. I'd only seen Ed four or five times before. We spoke every night by phone, but in terms of face-to-face contact, there hadn't been much. I didn't understand that when Ed gave me the watch, he assumed we were engaged. I'd given him a gold watch, as well, since my uncle was in that business, and I was able to pay for it in installments. To me, these were Valentine's Day gifts. Tokens of growing affection. No more, no less. Otherwise I would have been engaged to two people. John and I had never officially ended our engagement. I still had his grandmother's pearl ring. But I wasn't assertive enough to question Ed's decision. I told my parents, and they happily started planning the wedding. I thought to myself, "No one asked me. What about me? "But I was used to being invisible and kept my mouth shut. The wheels were in motion.

His mother decided to ignore the whole affair with the hope it would be canceled if she left the country. She and her husband left for a European vacation leaving my parents, who could not afford to pay for a ceremony, in charge of all the preparations. My parents borrowed money from our cousins (which ultimately Ed and I paid back) so the wedding could actually happen. Ed wasn't going to let his parents stop him. We were getting married whether they attended or not, whether they invited people or not, come hell or high water. Papa helped me put together a trousseau. Together, we made my entire wardrobe, some I designed myself. Some were designed by Papa. He made a couple of sleeveless dresses for me. He cut the patterns. He sewed some, I sewed some. Everything was, of course, impeccably tailored.

I needed a wedding dress, but there was no time to make one or to order one. Not that we could have afforded to order a gown. My brother's new girlfriend, Sylvia, worked in the fashion district, and her employer sold wedding gowns. Ilie and Sylvia took me to their warehouse. We saw a dress on a mannequin that was perfect, very simple, and it fit. Everything was coming together.

When Ed's parents realized the wedding was actually going to happen, they relented and returned from their vacation, handing Mutti a last-minute list of relatives who needed to be invited. They'd waited so late to participate, Mutti had to call people individually.

My friends quickly gave me a bridal shower, which meant a lunch. A few of the girls gave me nightgowns, which I had no intention of wearing, and my soon-to-be mother-in-law gave me a light-blue negligee with a robe. They were both see-through. I took one look at all the bows on the sleeves, and I threw it in the corner.

A few days before the wedding, I suddenly realized I couldn't cook or clean. I had not one domestic bone in my body. All my life, Mutti had done everything for me. I didn't even know how to iron. I knew what an iron looked like, but I'd never used one. This would not have been a problem except I had lied and told Ed I was a great cook. I told Mutti what I said, and we both panicked. She put me through a crash course on cooking, and I quizzed her and scribbled all her instructions on cards: "How to Make a Goulash." The food I hated as a child, wouldn't touch, I now desperately needed in order to prove my worth.

The morning of the wedding, the beauty salon put an amazing amount of curls in my hair. I didn't look like me. Mutti said, "You're going to wear that style?!" I put my head under the sink and combed it out. I plopped my veil on fairly damp hair, slathered on some lipstick, and headed to the Empire Hotel. It was a Jewish holiday, but the only day Ed had off the base. We found a reform rabbi who had served in the air force. He could relate to Ed's dilemma. He agreed to marry us.

At the ceremony, I walked in with Mutti and Papa, and I could see my mother-in-law, Ed's father, and his grandmother in the front row. They looked as if they were attending a funeral. Ed became nervous because his mother and grandmother were sobbing. It was ridiculous carrying on, with handkerchiefs and nose blowing and tears pouring down their faces. I was terrified Ed would change his mind when he saw their response. It upset him so badly, he started to sweat. As the rabbi asked us questions, I tried to concentrate, but was distracted by Ed staring at his parents in disbelief. He kept trying to make eye contact to signal to them, "Stop it!" Obviously, it didn't work. His mother and grandmother kept crying, but we forged ahead, stomped the glass, and were joined in holy matrimony. It took a very long time for Ed's mother to accept me as part of her family, and she only did so because Ed's younger brother married a woman who, as a child, had been horribly disfigured by polio. Suddenly, I wasn't such an abomination. His mother became much nicer to me, but it was too late, the damage had been done. I didn't trust her; I merely tolerated her. She was my elder, and I was polite, but I never forgot how she treated me in those early days. I never took her into my heart.

Ed and I, we couldn't have a real honeymoon. Ed had to report back to Texas five days later. We spent our wedding night in a Brooklyn hotel, and the next morning, I woke up, walked to the hotel salon, and instructed the stylist to cut off all my hair. She thought I was crazy, but I was not. I knew exactly how I felt, and I knew one thing for certain. I absolutely was not going to wake beside Ed every morning with a head full of rollers. I was shorn. I returned upstairs to our honeymoon room, and Ed nearly passed out at the sight of me. But, what was done was done. I knew my decision had very little to do with the inconvenience of rollers but I wasn't able to articulate my feelings. I had never had a voice and now, I had no hair.

Before we left for Texas, I returned home to say goodbye to Mutti and Papa. While I was there, the phone rang, and I answered it in my parents' bedroom. I couldn't believe what I heard. It was his voice. John was on the line. He said he'd been calling and calling. He swore he'd spoken with my brother, but Ilie wouldn't let me talk to him. He said he'd sent letters.

I felt my voice stick in my throat. "What letters?" Apparently, John's letters had been intercepted by my parents. It was like I'd been punched in the stomach. I couldn't breathe.

John said, "I love you. Why haven't you called me?"

I swallowed hard. "I just got married. I've been married for two days."

John started crying and yelling, "I'll never get married. I'll wait until you decide to change your mind. Maybe you'll get divorced. I'll wait as long as it takes!"

I had such strange horrible feelings. I didn't know what I felt anymore. I was nearly dizzy from the upset.

Outside the door, I heard Mutti say, "Where's Deborah?"

Then I heard Ed say, "Hey Deb? Are you still on the phone? Come in here already!"

I told John, "I'm sorry, but I can't talk to you."

He asked, "Don't you love me anymore?"

I said, "Yes, I do." I couldn't make sense of what was happening.

John yelled, "Please don't hang up! I love you!" but I had to hang up.

I went back into the living room, and everybody looked like strangers. I had the feeling I'd been sold. Not an arranged marriage by any means, but something was missing. I didn't feel like a wife. I felt like I had gone on a date and never come home.

Three days later, I was on a plane bound for Houston, Texas, with John's phone call nagging at me. I never tried to call him back. I never told my family or Ed that he called. Ed would have told him in no uncertain terms never to call me again. My parents would have been appalled. Papa would have ripped the phone off the wall. Deep down, I was hoping John would hunt me down. Then it wouldn't be my fault.

My first dinner cooking for Ed, I lied and told him I'd learned a few Chinese dishes while in Shanghai. I most certainly had not. I had to run out and buy canned Chinese food, dump it on plates, heat it, and throw parsley on top to make it look fresh. Ed loved the meal and wanted me to cook it again, but I'd tossed the can in the trash and couldn't remember the brand name. Fearful I'd purchase the wrong item, I talked him into German food, instead. I made a nice goulash since I had the actual recipe.

In Texas, I was alone all the time. Ed would be called out for maneuvers, and he had to grab his stuff and go. I never knew if he was coming home or not. I was alone without really being alone. I was married to a husband I never saw. Loneliness was a brand-new feeling. From the time I was three, I'd been living in one room on top of my entire family. It was cramped. I longed for privacy. I'd yearned for the day when I had more than a curtain to hide my secrets, but in all those years, I never realized that being constantly surrounded by family or classmates or even thousands of Chinese vendors and pedestrians felt safe. There were always people around. There was always noise, activity, and bustle. I knew Mutti always had her eye on me. Without her, without Papa, without Ilie and in the quiet of that military-wife life, I was miserable. I couldn't stand the isolation. I had complete separation anxiety.

Then three weeks into our marriage, I got pregnant. I told my parents. Mutti was thrilled to death. Papa was delighted. Ed told his parents. His mother collapsed from grief. Papa took it upon himself to yell at her, "Your response should have been congratulations!" From then on, she was afraid of Papa. Ed's own father never had the guts to talk back to her, ever, ever, ever. He liked that Papa stood up to his wife. He never said a word to Papa about it, but Mutti reprimanded me, "You've got to be respectful. After all, it's his mother. You can't keep her away from her own son."

Nobody was visiting us, anyway. My only company was a stray cat. Every time I opened the back door, there he was. I felt sorry for him and for myself so I put food out. For a while, he disappeared, and I started to miss him. Our neighbor had driven him out to a highway and dumped him, but he found his way back. I shouldn't have gotten attached. It was a terrible feeling. I didn't want to lose any more than I had already. I didn't want to spend more time mourning a loss like all those kittens in Shanghai. I'd become extremely attached to those kittens. They didn't talk back, and they were there for me. When they died . . . I didn't want to get into that position anymore. I didn't want to have anything die on me, but I didn't have that choice. I had a miscarriage.

The miscarriage brought with it not loss, but relief. I was twenty years old and not ready to have a child. I didn't want the responsibility of loving a stray cat, let alone a baby. I wasn't even sure how I'd ended up in Texas, by myself all day long, playing house with all the other military wives and wondering whether John ever thought about me. All my life I'd been rootless, stateless, but I'd never felt so displaced. So I was thrilled to hear, two months later, that my brother and Sylvia were unexpectedly getting married. It was the perfect excuse to leave that stray cat, Ed and go home . . . home to be with my family.

BROTHER

I was twenty-eight years old, having a great time when I started to feel that maybe I should marry. I was the only one of my friends still single, though in my defense, I'd been trying to find a job for a year and didn't have any money to date. When I finally got my job as a sketcher, a friend from Shanghai told me about a girl named Sylvia. She was working as a bookkeeper in the garment district. He thought we might have a lot in common. He suggested I call her. I asked her if she'd like to go to dinner or a movie or have lunch. She turned me down on all three counts.

A few weeks later, a mutual acquaintance threw a New Year's Eve party. I didn't want to go, but I got talked into it. Sylvia was there. She was very attractive with dark hair, nice eyes, and bangs. She wore glasses, had a pretty shape. We met, and we clicked. I liked that she was smart with a great sense of humor. I couldn't spend time with a woman whose interests were limited.

She admitted that she'd brushed me off because of my thick accent. She assumed I was short, old, bald, and fat. Then she saw me, and she changed her mind. I still had my red hair, blue eyes, and I looked fine. She may have turned me down on the phone, but I took her home that night. It was snowing so we took the subway to Avenue A and Fourth Street. Six months later, we got married.

I'd been running around enough, it was time to be with one person. Sylvia had dated someone seriously before me. I had dated serially not seriously. Something about her was different, though there was no great epiphany or revelation that convinced me to marry her. I'd grown up with my parents' attitudes toward affection. A word like "love" was never uttered during our upbringing. It was a European attitude even if I now lived in America.

So I didn't analyze my relationship with Sylvia. It was just knowing and knowing and then liking each other a lot and then falling in love and then me staying at her place every night and then getting married. We never even got engaged. We skipped that part. The closest we came to an engagement was me saying, "Maybe we should put this on a more permanent basis."

Sylvia looked at me, oddly. "You mean get married?"

I said, "Okay." That was my proposal. There was no reason not to marry. She laughed at my jokes.

Our quick decision to marry took my family a bit by surprise, but Papa liked Sylvia. He respected her no-nonsense attitude and her work ethic. He liked that she had integrity, and he could tell that she had a business mind. Sylvia could be a bit reserved, a bit distant. She'd had a difficult childhood. Her mom was a small woman who had polio as a child. Her father was a handsome man, but a brutal alcoholic. He was abusive, and though they weren't divorced, her father didn't stay home most nights. She wasn't close with them. She'd moved out years earlier, living on her own in Manhattan, very independent for that day and age. She had to be to have survived the kind of family she had. I loved that she was independent. I loved that she was smart. It's part of why I found her so appealing. But Sylvia assumed that most families weren't happy ones. It took her a while to warm up to Mutti and Papa, to know what it meant to be part of a close family.

As for the wedding, we hated it. We wanted a simple wedding, but her family insisted on throwing a gigantic affair maybe to make up for all that had been done. Having made only obligatory visits to her parents, it came as a surprise to Sylvia that for our wedding, they went full-court press. They rented a hall, and there was dancing and food coming from every direction, the families were kissing and hugging. It was quite a show. At first, Sylvia was very uncomfortable with the whole rigmarole, but she finally allowed herself to enjoy the spirit of the day. She took off her shoes and danced.

We spent a week in Provincetown for our honeymoon, and when we returned, we moved into an apartment on the parlor floor of a brownstone on Eighty-second Street between Amsterdam and Columbus that had belonged to the critic Lewis Mumford. It had high ceilings and a brick wall. We were happy there. Sylvia took a job as an office manager, and I returned to my job as a sketcher for Mr. Mangone. Every day, we met for lunch in the garment district to exchange complaints about our jobs. The unbelievable incompetence of fellow workers, the stupidity of bosses.

It was not long after our honeymoon that Mutti called, frantic. Papa had collapsed in the kitchen and couldn't get up. I rushed over to help get him to the hospital. Papa had a stroke. All those years of scraping by and malnutrition and wondering when the next suit might be ordered, the stress of losing his home, his business, his reputation, his pride, it finally took its toll. The doctors warned us there would be changes, still I wasn't prepared.

Papa became meek and quiet. He stopped arguing, and for the first time in my life, I saw my father scared. He wouldn't be able to work anymore, and he could no longer walk without the assistance of a cane. All his life, he had strutted through the world with an arrogance that protected him. The stroke stole his confidence. It took away his bravado. He wasn't the same man. It was heartbreaking.

SISTER

Seeing everyone at Ilie's wedding, I got homesick. I thought maybe I could wait out the rest of Ed's tour by staying in New York. Frankly, I wasn't even sure I wanted to be married. I called Ed and told him I needed to stay a little bit longer. I said Mutti was lonesome without me, and with Ilie leaving, I felt it best to spend more time with her. A few days later, I called and delayed my flight once again. Twelve days after that, Mutti got suspicious. She thought Ed didn't want me to come back. She didn't understand why every time I was scheduled to go on a flight, it was changed to another day, another day. I kept postponing. She finally cornered me. I admitted, "I don't like Houston that much. Maybe I could stay here a little bit longer?"

Mutti loved Ed, and she felt that my rightful place was by his side. She packed me quickly, made sure the tickets were rescheduled, then she and Papa took me to the airport. They pretty much marched me to the plane door. Mutti told the airline stewardess, "Will you please make sure she stays on the plane?"

I returned to Texas and suffered through one more year only to learn that Ed was being transferred to Knob Noster in Missouri, population tiny. Houston had been isolating, but Knob Noster was downright rural. The town doctor not only delivered babies, he also served as the local veterinarian. In 1958, when I discovered I was pregnant again, there was no way I was going to let a vet deliver my son. Ed got an extension to get off base, and we headed back to New York.

It was the longest I'd been away from my family, ever, and I was shocked to see Papa was now walking with a cane. He seemed different. Quiet. Much less active. I was truly concerned. I asked Mutti, "Why is Papa using a cane?"

Reverting to yet another one of her great lies to protect me, Mutti told me, "He hurt his foot."

All right, he hurt his foot. I believed her. Why would I think anything else?

I was much too bashful and quiet to protest when Ed's mother insisted we visit his grandmother in Woodbridge, New Jersey, even though I wanted to spend time with my own parents and not his family. I believed I had to be polite to my elders even if I disliked them immensely. Ed must have said something to his mother about me wanting time with my parents because his mother announced, "If your parents want to join us, fine, but that's what we will be doing." I asked my parents to join us for the drive. Just as we were about to get in the car, my father-in-law insisted on snapping a photo. He was always taking pictures. I had no idea, at the moment, my entire life was about to change.

Three hours into our drive, Papa got a strange look on his face. He said, "My head hurts."

Mutti started to scream. It didn't make any sense for her to scream like that.

I tried to calm her. "Mutti, don't you have an aspirin? Papa has a headache."

Then Papa keeled over in my lap.

My mother-in-law turned around to see what was happening. The first words out of her mouth were, "Everything happens on our vacation."

Ed's father pulled the car to a stop. I said to Ed, "I've got to get out." He thought I was going to throw up, but I saw a synagogue. I ran toward the temple with Ed chasing after me. I ran inside, wearing shorts and a short-sleeve shirt. The temple was Orthodox, and the rabbi told me it was disrespectful for me to enter. I tried to explain that my father had just collapsed in my lap but, he wouldn't listen to me. He said, "Come back when you're dressed appropriately." I walked out, in a state of shock. Ed was waiting for me on the stairs. I told him, "I will never set foot in a temple again."

We walked back to the car. Ed called for an ambulance, and they finally arrived to take Papa. The next thing I knew, we were at the hospital, and Papa was in a coma inside an iron lung on life support. I stood by the door. I couldn't even walk into his room. I watched Mutti as if she were moving through another world. Ed tried to hug me, but I brushed him off. I told him, "There's no problem." Papa died before Ilie could make it to the hospital. All that was left was his suit, hanging over the arm of a chair.

Papa did not believe in insurance policies. He said it was an American way of life. "Insurance? Why take insurance? That's American! That's stupid!" Mutti finally had to tell me the truth. She had to admit he'd had an earlier stroke and that she'd chosen not to tell me for fear I would pull a repeat performance of my post-Ilie's-wedding refusal to fly home. She knew I was having a hard time adjusting to marriage. She also knew I would run home to be by Papa's side. She wanted to protect me from the bad news and give me a moment to enjoy life with Ed. She wanted me to be happy. She didn't want to burden me. She was worried she wouldn't be able to get me back on a plane again. None of her excuses brought me any peace.

Especially when I learned that Papa wasn't supposed to take any long trips. The Jersey trip was a good three hours. Distraught, I asked her, "Then why did you let him go?"

Mutti explained, "I told Ed's mother that he was very frail, but she said, 'So don't go.' Your father wanted to see you. He's very stubborn."

Hearing this, I blamed my in-laws for my father's death. They knew he wasn't well, and yet, they had insisted we go. Their thoughtlessness had put him in that car in the first place.

"He's been sick for months and months," Ilie told me. He thought I knew. Clearly, I didn't, and neither of us knew that the money was drained. Papa's poor health had taken every dime. There was no money to bury my father. I'd never felt so low in my life. To be that poor, unable to bury Papa. It was worse than Shanghai. Our cousin discreetly handed me a blank check to cover the expenses.

The funeral was a traditional Jewish ceremony. Ilie and Sylvia stood in front with Mutti. I hovered all the way in the back. I didn't want to get too close. I'd seen dead bodies in China, plenty of them, but Papa, seeing Papa dead, that was impossible. I couldn't deal with it. I wanted to run away.

We sat Shiva for a few days in the apartment, but I refused to spend the nights there. Even though Papa died in the hospital, I was spooked. His cane and his glasses were by his bedside, and it made my arms fill with goose bumps. At night, after leaving Mutti, my mind spun constantly. What if there hadn't been a war, and what if I'd been allowed to grow up in Austria where I was born? Would Papa have lived longer? Would I have gotten married? I never would have spoken English. What would my life have been like? To live as a European.

I became certain that Papa would not have had a stroke so early in his life if he could have lived his life in a fair Vienna. He had no control. No real choice. His only choice was death or leave, but in leaving, he lost everything. All those years of trying to get to America . . . was it worth it to finally make it to New York? He gained his freedom of speech, but that was never a freedom Papa surrendered. What he needed was the freedom to eat, to work. The freedom from incessant struggle. He left both Vienna and China because he was forced out. America had always seemed like the Promised Land, but it wasn't the dream he'd expected. We hadn't been saved. He couldn't speak the language, he couldn't make the living he needed to support us, and he would not take money from anybody. He'd rather we didn't eat, which we didn't. Papa had been well respected, even in China, and all of a sudden, he was working in a factory, sewing seams. It broke his spirit. It hastened his death.

His death changed me profoundly. I'd always been shy. Now I retreated into myself, second-guessing every word, every gesture, every plan. If somebody told me they were having a party, I wouldn't even bother getting dressed. Papa had had a stroke, and Mutti chose not to call me. She had lied by omission, and I'd lost all that time with Papa as a result. It would take me another ten years to be able to talk about Papa in the past tense, but it only took a heartbeat for me to never trust anyone again.

BROTHER

To lose Papa affected me deeply. There was a great sense of loss about conversations that never happened. We had never talked about our relationship. We never had father/son discussions. I don't even know what those conversations would have entailed. I just had the sense they should have taken place. There was a hole between us. I felt it profoundly. I wished I'd been able to tell him that I appreciated him, that I loved him. I never said that to him. I was in my twenties, old enough to regret what hadn't been done. I should have. I could have. Why didn't I? Even at that age, I felt gratitude for him. I never verbalized my gratitude for the way he supported me during my job search. Why hadn't I said it out loud?

The last image in my mind, as I left the hospital, was his shirt and pants folded neatly on a chair, his socks and shoes underneath. It still haunts me.

After his death, Sylvia and I both took a leave of absence from our jobs and drove across country. We bought a Volvo when nobody had Volvos. You saw a Volvo on the road, you tooted at each other. We spent the summer driving from New York across Kansas to Denver then through Santa Fe to Gallup, New Mexico. We went to Las Vegas. Being too snobby to go to Los Angeles, we went to Bakersfield, instead. We headed north from there. We kept hearing about the great northern California beaches. Great beaches, yeah, but the water was ice cold! We had to drive back across the Badlands to get to Cape Cod so we could swim. The water on the Cape was immeasurably warmer.

We returned to our jobs in New York. My boss, Philip Mangone died, and his daughter took over the business. She hired another designer. He was Spanish, a tall, handsome man who couldn't sketch, but she was taken with him. I saw the handwriting on the wall, and sure enough, in the spring, she let me go. It was the best thing that happened to me.

I got my first job as an actual designer for Seymour Fox. He'd been in the business for years. It was an old, good house established by his father. We only made suits for women. Expensive suits. Seymour Fox was a man very much taken with his looks. His tailors kept big iron pieces for pressing the clothes onto their ironing boards. Seymour would walk into the cutting room, pick up the irons, and lift them as if they were weights, do shoulder presses with them. He was a vain man, but a nice guy.

Even though I was the designer, Seymour had the ultimate say as to what would be shown to the customers.

He took me to Paris to work the shows. My first trip back was quite different, particularly as I progressed from student to an expense account. Seymour and I spent all our days looking at clothes, attending all the major collections, looking for items we could use. Since most collections focused on glamorous, sumptuous concoctions to keep a blasé press awake, finding something that would appeal to our customers was like looking for a needle in a haystack. After much agonizing, we listed some numbers and returned the next morning to review. Invariably, there would be a letdown. In the show, beautiful, sexy models, slinking down the runway, with all the makeup and accessories, the clothes looked fabulous—not so much on the hanger—they looked slightly forlorn. But since we were committed to buy, I was always able to find something I could use. We weren't supposed to take these pieces and make exact copies; we were supposed to use them for inspiration, which we did.

I never considered the shows at Seymour Fox to be truly my shows. They weren't. They were his. When my cousins asked if I wanted to go into business for myself, of course, I said yes. They had made a lot of money and thought they could put me into business. They said, "We can do anything. Don't worry about the customers!" So I didn't worry about the customers.

My first show was in my showroom at 530 Seventh Avenue in the center of the Garment District. I showed suits, coats, dresses, and jackets. I had the best coats. Classic style. I didn't believe in over-ornamentation. It was all about proportion. The lapel, the length, the color, the quality of the fabric, the tailoring. I believe when a woman puts on a coat, she shouldn't feel it. It should feel natural. There should be no struggle. If it's tight in the armhole, that's not good. I knew how a coat should rest on the body, a protective extension of one's self. I made coats with as few seams as possible. Not an easy feat.

My models were tall, between five feet nine inches or five feet ten inches and a size six or eight. For coats, you need human coat hangers, basically. Coat hangers that know how to walk. Shoulders, they had to have broad shoulders. No bosoms, that didn't matter. Faces. Good faces. Modeling can't be taught. All those modeling schools that advertise they will make your daughter a model, it's a scam. I had a girl who worked for me one summer. She wasn't a model, but she'd put on a coat and she just instinctively knew how to walk. It was all there. Nobody had to tell her. A sense of fashion, how to move, how to project. That's what I looked for in a girl.

I showed about seventy pieces and sold thirty-five or forty. My clothes had oomph to them. I wanted people to recognize them. They had a signature look created by fit and structure. Of course, I had no idea what coat would actually sell. It was a crapshoot. Out of those forty, if I had five hot numbers, I was doing well. The one that did best was a fitted coat that had a half-belt in the front with a knot closing, much like a knot button on a Chinese silk dress, the same principle. The coat had nice, big lapels, a standing collar. It had a lot of dash to it.

The idea was to sell as few styles as possible, but as many pieces of each of those selected styles. The more you cut, the less the production costs. It was very different than my father's business. He was a custom tailor, and in comparison, I was in the wholesale business though I had a limited customer base. There was only a small group of women who could afford my clothes, but enough to keep me in business. I didn't have to sell thousands. I did well if I sold three to four hundred of a style. Volume wasn't my concern. I was a small operation, but I got great press from *Women's Wear Daily*. I was considered a new young designer. I was up and coming. I was emerging. I had my name on the door. I was "new blood" until we started hemorrhaging. My cousins had no connections. There weren't enough customers. Money went like water. It lasted for two years before my cousins pulled the plug. We were done, finished. Closing up shop. It seemed my days as a designer with my own name on the door were through.

I was oddly calm about the whole debacle. Having survived Shanghai, I knew I could survive anything. I could survive without the business. It was great to have it, but I didn't need it. I needed very little money on which to live. Shanghai had toughened me. It stayed in my subconscious. I came out not needing much from life. A roof over my head, a little food, a place to run, maybe some paints. Those years in Shanghai created in me a self-reliance that kept me grounded in an industry that was infamous for destroying dreams and careers in the blink of an eye. I never took the business of fashion seriously. The craft, yes, but the business was tongue in cheek. I maintained a distance from it. I never wanted to be part of the inner clique. I was the only fashion designer I knew who hated to shop. So the business shuttered, and I walked away with my head held high.

Sylvia got pregnant that last year I was on my own. It was planned. We'd been married for eight years without children. We'd been traveling and having a great time. We both made decent money. All our friends had kids. There comes a point of no return. You get older, you don't want to deal with babies. You don't have the patience. You need to be young to handle children. It was time.

Sylvia worked until the day she was due. I made a maternity dress for her. It was an A-line dress with pockets and a simple neckline that didn't look like a typical maternity dress at that time. It was stylish in a market filled with frumpy muumuus. The buyer for Henri Bendel saw it and loved it so much she ordered sixty pieces.

I'd already shut down my operations, so I had to hunt down a place to have the dresses made, and in the midst of my hunt, my daughter was born. We named her Maris, after Papa, an adaptation of his name, Moritz. It was a name that confused our family members. When I called my cousin to give him the great news, there was a brief silence before he said in Yiddish, "As long as she's healthy." It took me a long time to realize people thought we'd named her after the baseball player Roger Maris. I wasn't a baseball fan. It was a reference that went right over my head.

Sylvia and I, we liked the name Maris. We liked it so much we named that maternity dress the Maris. It's out there somewhere, on eBay, forty years later.

SISTER

Since walking the stage as Miss Vienna, Mutti had never been alone. She'd married Papa, given birth to Ilie, to me, and for decades, had functioned as the glue that held us all together. Then I got married and had a nine-pound, four-ounce baby boy, Mark, Ilie got married, and Papa was gone. Mutti was on her own. It worried me.

Ed and I invited her to stay with us. At first, I was concerned, "What if when she gets off the plane and she cries all the time?" How would I handle that? I didn't want to see Mutti cry. I shouldn't have fretted. When Mutti got off the plane, I was flabbergasted. She was wearing a navy suit with a white blouse. She was stunning. I'd convinced myself that Mutti had become a broken-down woman who wouldn't be able to deal with Papa's death. This gorgeous woman got off the plane, dressed extremely well, upbeat. I exclaimed, "Mutti, you actually flew!" She was terrified of flying. She said, "Yes, I don't care. Okay, I'll die, so I'll fly."

Mutti had spent her entire life being scared. Frightened in Vienna. Frightened in China. Frightened in Canada. Frightened in New

York. Always about Papa and his high blood pressure. If Papa found out this or that or did this or that, he would get a stroke and die. Mutti basically mourned his death for years. She mourned him while he was alive. She felt liberated from the fear of worrying about his death. Not quite relief, but it gave her a chance to breathe. Her spirit changed. She was lighter.

She stayed with us for a year, and she was upbeat the entire time. Every time I turned around to do something in the house, laundry or washing the car, everything was done already. She was such a help with the baby. She felt she had to earn her keep. She never could just sit and visit, sit and wait. She didn't talk much about Papa. Whenever she referred to him, she'd still call him by his last name. "Wacs did this. Wacs did that." It was like having my best girlfriend come live with me. I wanted her to stay longer, but Mutti had other plans.

She decided to go back to work. She hadn't worked in years! She made garter belts and slippers for brides, but it wasn't enough to keep her afloat. Ilie was supporting her financially. Mutti absolutely did not want to be dependent on my brother. When she found a man willing to support her, she married him purely to alleviate my brother from having to write a monthly check. It had nothing to do with love.

Walter was a widower, and Mutti was, at that time, fifty-six. He insisted, "You can't be more than forty-six." So she took ten years off her age and stayed with that so adamantly that she never collected Social Security. As a result of her ongoing fib, there had to be a lot of silent mathematics done in everybody's head especially when I tagged along. I had to keep lowering my own age to keep up with Mutti's stories. It got to the point where it would have been impossible for me to have ever been born! Vanity was very big on Mutti's list, and it was contagious.

In the early '60s, Ed and I moved back to New Jersey a few doors down from Mutti. Her new husband was quite possessive and jealous that she spent so much time with us. He got very uptight when I became pregnant and had my second son, Mitchell, another big boy weighing in at eight pounds, six ounces. Mutti would be on her way over, and he would suddenly get a headache. Mutti was never the kind of woman to say, "I'm sorry, my daughter comes first."

Walter was the head of a plumbing company. Could he fix a sink? I don't know, but he made good money. Mutti never wanted for anything. Then again, Mutti wasn't demanding. Even though he had a heart condition, he was miserly and wouldn't spend the money on a car with air conditioning. Eventually, he had a heart attack. As the ambulance rolled him away, he pointed to Mutti and yelled, "It's her fault." If I'd been her, I would have left right then and there. She loved alpha men. Maybe Mutti married Papa to get out of her sister's house and not be dependent on her sister the same way she married Walter so she wouldn't be dependent on Ilie. Maybe Walter was less of a convenience and more of a repetition.

He always told heroic stories. "Someone almost died, and he had to rescue, blah, blah, blah." Ed viewed him as a stupid man. When he'd visit, Ed would read the newspaper. He refused to have a conversation with him. Walter found Ed rude, but that was Ed. There was no changing either of them. At least, Walter wasn't a yeller like Papa.

Then Mutti was diagnosed with cancer. After treatment, she went into remission and was doing great until she started to cough. I begged her to go to the doctor, but she didn't believe in babying herself. Ultimately, I insisted, and it turned out she had walking pneumonia. They treated her, and she was about to be released. We went to the hospital to visit her, and at the end of our chatting, Ed drove me home.

When we got back to the house, I told Ed, "I have this feeling we shouldn't go out tonight. We should just stay put." I said, "Something's wrong with Mutti." He said, "I'll take you back if you want." It was about a forty-five-minute ride. He said, "She'll wonder why we're back again. I think you'll upset her." I agreed to stay home on the condition we wouldn't go out. Nothing happened. Then, at two o'clock in the morning, I woke up and walked into the kitchen. I stayed there until the phone rang at six o'clock. I didn't even wait for Ed to say hello. I got the vacuum, plugged it in, and vacuumed. I needed the noise, so I wouldn't hear anything. Mutti had died at two a.m.

Ed called Ilie to come over. I was just angry. I said, "Don't touch me! Don't hold me! What do you want? Go away, I'm fine!" I just wanted to clean. I wouldn't stop. I made Ed go to the hospital to make sure it was Mutti. I hoped maybe they made a mistake. Ed and Ilie went, and they confirmed that yes, it was her. Mutti was gone.

I'm the only person I know who can go to a funeral, have the person you love the most in the world die, and not cry. At Mutti's funeral, I wore sunglasses because I didn't want anybody to see me tear up. When Ed tried to put his arm around me, I shoved him away. Her death was very, very difficult for me. I couldn't talk about her. I couldn't see any pictures. I certainly couldn't go visit her grave.

Walter insisted she not be buried beside Papa. Papa had an empty plot beside him, but Walter was so heartbroken when Mutti died, crying and carrying on, that I figured funerals are for the living. I couldn't force him to put Mutti next to Papa. He loved her, so what was the difference? Dead is dead. We let Walter do it his way, but I made sure we didn't put down the real date of her birth on the death certificate. While I couldn't control Walter, I could make sure Mutti's vanity was honored.

After Mutti passed away, we treated her husband like a father. We had him over every day. He always told Ed, "There's a will, and I'm leaving everything to you both. Ed, you will be the executor." We both said we didn't want to hear about it. Walter then got it into his head that he needed to go to Romania. Mutti had been corresponding with Papa's brother who helped us escape Austria by paying for the passage on the Italian ship. They'd become very close over the years, and Mutti never had the chance to actually meet him in person. Walter wanted to go to Romania just to thank the people Mutti loved so dearly. Ed and I bought him a plane ticket. We figured he didn't have the money to go. We waved goodbye and sent him on his way with a "Have a good time."

A week or two later, a government representative came knocking on my door. "Walter died in a communist country." I nearly fainted and grabbed at the railing on the stairs. I felt as if I'd been transported into a war movie or a spy movie and that we would soon be in big trouble. I had to have the man explain again what happened. There was no great mystery. Walter had had yet another heart attack only this time he was overseas, and it was fatal. We had no idea how to handle the body. I called Ilie, who spoke the language better than I, and he found out we had to pay $5,000 to get Walter's body back to the United States. Plus, it had to be done in a way where nobody could know, and we could never open the coffin. It would be sealed so tightly shut that even a funeral parlor wouldn't be able to open it. I told Ilie, "How do we know we're not getting Mussolini back?" Frankly, we didn't, still Ilie fronted the money as Ed and I began making arrangements to bury Mutti's second husband.

That's when Ed remembered, "Didn't Walter say he left a will? Maybe there's some money there to defray these costs." We went to his apartment and searched the place. We found the will in the oven with a bunch of keys and a bank name. Ed assumed the keys were for safe-deposit boxes, so we drove over to the bank. I sat in the car for a long time waiting for Ed to come out, but he didn't. I thought, "How long does it take to open the damn box?" I walked inside.

I found Ed surrounded by a lot of people from the bank. He was actually perspiring. When he opened the first box, it contained socks filled with silver dollars. I saw that and started to cry, which truly shocked Ed. I wasn't one to show emotion, but I felt so sorry for Walter. Seeing those socks filled with silver dollars touched my heart. As it turned out, my tears were premature. There were other keys. One key led to another box then another box then another box.

Walter had amassed a fortune in money and stocks. Ed kept sweating and counting. I couldn't understand. We had just paid for Walter's trip because he didn't have any money. He'd been rich the whole time? Ed finally stopped counting and said, "Ilie can close his doors right now, there's so much money. This is wealth unbelievable." Ed asked the bank if he could get a room to make a private call. He called Ilie and said, "There are stacks and stacks of deposits. Each box has more boxes. There's a bank we haven't even gotten to yet." As he's telling my brother, Ed started reading the will. Walter had changed his will after Mutti died. He made Ed the executor, but he left everything to his sister. We didn't even know he had a sister; he hadn't spoken to her in over forty years. Ed paused and said, "Well, we were rich."

We had to find the sister. We didn't even know her name. We knew Walter was originally from Austria so we went to the Austrian consulate. They could confirm he had a sister in Austria, but they didn't know where she lived. When Walter's lawyer told Ed the expenses for a trip to find the sister would be covered by his estate, we bought two plane tickets and headed to Vienna.

I'd always wanted to visit the place where I was born. I used to feel envious of friends who told me, "Oh, I've lived in this house for thirty years, and I was raised here." I wanted that same experience, to grow up in the place where I was born rather than be shipped from one country to another. Ed couldn't understand why I still considered Vienna my homeland after all we'd suffered. Ilie had told him the stories I wouldn't. Ed had stronger feelings against the city than I did, and he'd lived a semi-luxurious life in the United States! I couldn't explain it, either. Vienna felt like home.

Though I was eager to see my homeland, I certainly didn't want to go back to give away a fortune. I told Ed, "We could say we didn't find her."

He said, "I like to sleep at night."

I said, "I'll sleep a lot better if we keep the money."

Ed insisted, "We need to do this correctly." So we packed our bags.

We landed in Austria, and the first thing I wanted to see was the Ferris wheel of the Prater. It was exactly as I remembered it, still overwhelming and still shaped like the front tire of a giant's bicycle. I walked through the Prater and tried to conjure wonderful memories. Memories that weren't mine to conjure. I was aware of what I was doing, but still, I did it.

When I stood in front of the building that replaced the apartment where we had lived, it was like finding a lost city. As if I was standing among the ruins of my history, my own personal Pompeii. I felt comforted. It resonated through me. This is where my parents were, and this is where I had been. I could imagine Mutti standing on that exact sidewalk next to me. She would have been emotional seeing all the things that had changed. It would have been sad for her finding the place she lived with her sister. I didn't know where that building was. It would have brought back a lot of memories for her. Had I been standing on that sidewalk alone, without Ed, I probably would have lingered for hours.

I was retracing my parents' footsteps. It made me feel closer to them. As if their presence was with me, a connection to them I didn't feel in the United States. In America, I felt their death. In Vienna, I had a sense of their life, of their spirits as if they were looking down on me. For the first time, I wanted to believe in the hereafter. I wanted to believe my parents could be reincarnated. Maybe they had to be poverty stricken during the life we'd shared, but next time around, they would get to be royalty.

Ed was amazed at how comfortable I was. I was extremely relaxed. I almost looked happy. I loved asking for directions—anything, to speak the language. I loved speaking German. I wanted to cling to the language because my parents spoke it, it was ours, and it had never been taken away even if I would never be considered a Viennese citizen.

I acted as his tour guide. I loved ordering food that wasn't on the menu. Food I wouldn't touch as a kid, now I craved. It was the food Mutti described when she spoke of castles and a faraway land. Food that represented the childhood of my dreams. A childhood I never had, that never existed. I had to have the flourless dark chocolate cake with raspberry jelly, chocolate icing, and whipped cream on top. I had to have pork with vinegar and onions. I wanted the authentic tastes I'd never been able to experience in China with mothers trying to replicate German dishes on hibachi flowerpot grills. I could not remember any of these foods from my infancy in Vienna, and Mutti's descriptions of them paled in comparison to an actual bite in my mouth. My taste buds longed for home. Even if the home was just a fantasy.

Ilie would have been appalled at my behavior, admiring the Viennese as if they had not kicked us out, murdered our family, and wildly cheered while doing so. He would have shaken his head, thrown up his hands, and told me I was glorifying a past I never knew. All I'd ever known was our poverty in China. The fantasies I held about Vienna were by-products of Mutti's storytelling that had taken hold. Ilie would just as well never been born there in the first place. He would have been happy to be born in China. His bad memories outweighed the good ones. In my opinion, the younger generation in Vienna had nothing to do with my past, and I wasn't about to hold them accountable for the sins of their parents. I didn't experience anti-Semitism while there. Had I seen a swastika or any remnant of that hatred, it would have broken my heart in two. I felt more at home in the company of the Austrians than I did anywhere else in the world. I understood that it made no sense. I knew I was more wrong than right to embrace the country as my homeland, but I couldn't make that comforting feeling go away, and I didn't want to.

We weren't there for a sightseeing tour, anyway. The purpose of our trip was not nostalgic. We'd come to find Walter's sister. We began searching for the buildings where she used to live. Finally, in one apartment, a woman opened the door, and she looked exactly like

Walter. When she saw us, she nearly slammed the door in our faces. She thought we wanted something. I spoke German and explained why we were there. Then, she was friendly. She told us that when Walter, her brother, was a young boy, he made a promise to his dying parents. He would always take care of his sister. For forty years, he ignored her, but once dead, he'd finally fulfilled his promise.

In the meantime, Walter's body, or perhaps Mussolini's body, was being shipped to the United States for a burial. We tried to stop them from loading him on the plane. It was too late, he was on his way.

The will allowed for all the costs of the funeral to come off the top with the remainder to go to the sister. We decided the heck with it. We were going to give Walter a great send-off. We got the biggest hearse we could find. We didn't give a damn who the hell was in that coffin. It didn't even matter. We knew he had to be dead, or else he'd have his fingers tightly gripped around all that money.

At the funeral home, I'd never seen so many people. He was a charismatic man and friendly to everyone. Pretty much every clerk from every department store and supermarket showed. We sat there and pretended we were sad with people telling us what a loss, how wonderful a man Walter had been. Sylvia leaned over to me and whispered, "Son of a bitch."

After the services, Ilie asked us all, "Why are we burying him next to Mutti?" The hole was already prepped, but once the question had been asked, none of us wanted to put him beside Mutti. I had an idea. I said, "Let's bury him next to Papa. Papa can give him hell." In the end, we decided against a vindictive burial, though when I go to visit Mutti, I stand on Walter's grave. It brings me an odd sensation of peace.

BROTHER

I had to find a new job. I had my name, not much else, but that was enough. The industry knew who I was, and now they came to me. I could pick from a couple of offers, and I picked Originala. I became their head designer. It was a big operation. I had four designing rooms that produced eight lines a year: two early spring lines, two late spring lines, two early fall lines, and two late fall lines. All we made was outerwear, coats and suits.

I had four patternmakers who each had four tailors working for them. Unless a patternmaker had a sketch, he couldn't make a pattern, and there was nothing to feed to the tailors. I'd been hired on a trial basis. I had no idea how I was going to keep up. I'd make sketches and show them to the boss, Nat Bader. He'd say, "We've had this before. This is not what we want. We want something else." He'd tell me to look at what we were already doing and to give him something just a little bit different. I'd go back, make new sketches, and he'd say, "It's not different enough." I decided the job wasn't going to last anyway. To hell with it. I would do whatever I thought was right, and if he didn't like it, he could fire me. I stopped agonizing over sketches and just learned to feed the patternmakers. I stopped submitting sketches entirely and just made the coats, showing them to Nat only when they were finished, minus the buttons. Nat liked to pick buttons. It made him happy. Fine with me. Nat was happy. His brother, Irving, was happy, but most importantly, the customers were happy. Suddenly, I was a hero.

I went with Nat to Paris, Italy, and Spain twice a year for the collections in January and in July. In Rome, we stayed at the Hilton on the hill. One trip, I flew into Rome around six in the morning, and they had no reservation under my name. I was standing at the check-in desk looking lost when a friend of Nat's, a big-time manufacturer, Mr. P., came to my rescue. He was a big, rough-around-the-edges guy.

Mr. P. asked, "What's the matter, kid?" I told him they didn't have a room for me. He called over the manager and yelled, "Give the kid a fucking room for Christ's sakes!" The manager meekly replied, "Yes sir!" Suddenly, there was a room for me. Mr. P. turned to me and said, "You've got to know how to talk to these guys."

Paris was much more fun with Originala. We went to all of the shows: Dior, Valentino, Yves St. Laurent, and Courrèges. Nat Bader may have been self-centered, but he understood there was a lot of fluff in the world of fashion. Paris was hallowed ground, haute couture was presented in cathedral silence, models would walk with stately pace, disdainful expressions on their faces, bestowing upon us, the undeserved, a privilege. Nat and I, we decided their shoes were too tight. We both approached our business with a fine sense of Yiddish humor. Neither of us took ourselves that seriously.

I met Gloria Emerson, a writer who covered fashion for *The New York Times*. She became a close friend to Sylvia and me. (Later, she would cover the war in Vietnam for the *Times*.) At that time, the press was not allowed to view the collections for another two months. The press depended on the American buyers for vital information, for instance: whether hems were coming up or down; shoulders wider or narrower.

At our buying appointments, Nat suddenly hated everything. He'd walk into Balenciaga's showroom and yell, "I bought this coat last year!" His saleslady would protest, "No, monsieur. Look at these seams." He'd yell back, "What seams? Same coat!" We went to Courrèges, who was a big name at that time. He'd been a tailor at Balenciaga, and he made beautiful clothes. Nat did not speak French, so I had to serve as translator. Nat would gesture toward a coat. "Tell him the neckline is wrong." I was horrified. I told Nat, "You tell him!" Since he had no patience, I had to make the decisions. I bought what I liked. I loved Balenciaga. He made coats I could relate to, classic, beautifully constructed, and tailored. He changed the silhouette for suits and boxy coats. St. Laurent, I liked a lot, as well. He was an innovator, but I couldn't find much to buy from him. He was mostly dresses, though he did launch the women's tuxedo and turned a Navy peacoat into high fashion.

The coats arrived a month later in New York, and Nat would huff, "This is what we bought!" though I could usually get some use out of them. We kept them for a couple of weeks, and then we'd sell them in Canada. We had a manufacturer there who bought from us. We copied the coat immediately to have a record of it, and then I would make changes.

Most of the manufacturers, when the big stores came in, they were quite subservient; they would do anything to please them. When the little stores came in, the manufacturers played the big shots. Nat was an equal-opportunity abuser. He didn't care if you were big or little, he told you what to buy. There was a time frame. You had to commit yourself to get delivery on time. No matter who it was, he wouldn't budge an inch. I liked that about him.

It was during one of those buying trips to Paris that I returned to Austria for the first time since the war. Walter, the shirt maker's son who'd accompanied me every evening for a walk around the prison or to defend our turf against the White Russians, had settled back in Vienna with his parents. Before the war, his father owned a haberdashery. The older generation, our parents, were always looking to go back to Vienna. They never left it in their hearts. They re-created a culture in Shanghai that was an amalgamation of Berlin and Vienna. When Walter's father had the chance to reclaim his old business, he took it and insisted that his son come work for him. Walter had been a brilliant boy, was still a brilliant man who could have done many different things with his life, but his father felt his place was in the family business.

The thought of setting foot in Vienna made my skin crawl, but I hadn't seen my old friend in many years. I caved in and took him up on his offer to host me for a weekend visit. I revisited the old places. Our street was still there. The building was gone. It struck me how small Vienna was. I held a memory of the city being much bigger than it actually was. I'd been a little kid. The streets were not big boulevards. They were small streets. I had perceived it from a child's vision.

Austria was still living in denial. My friend, Bob, had gone back to Vienna earlier to visit an uncle. The uncle took him to see his old apartment. He knocked on the door and explained how he used to live there. The current residents thought he came to claim it. They were hostile. "We didn't take it away from you!" They slammed the door shut.

There was only one Jewish museum, which was pathetic, and there were no memorials to mark what happened. I knew I couldn't hold the sons accountable for the sins of the fathers. The problem was there were just too many fathers and grandfathers still around. It put a damper on my visit. I had no grief with the young people, but if I saw someone who had a couple of years on me, I had to wonder what they were doing during the war.

I wasn't comfortable there. I didn't want to be. The Viennese German came back to me, and I started to feel as if I'd never left. I didn't like that feeling. I didn't want to speak German. I have a visceral rejection to that city. To me, it had a superficial look. If Disney had created Vienna, this is what they would have made. Architecture with curlicues. On and on and on and cabbage all over the place and horses beside horses and men on horses with shields and armor. There was nothing in Vienna I couldn't see in Paris. I didn't need to come to peace with that place. I was done with it. It was the past, and I still hated it all. I asked Walter, "How can you live here? There's anti-Semitism." He said "Yes, there's anti-Semitism here, but you also have anti-Semitism in the United States." I argued, "Maybe so, but you can live your whole life in the U.S. without ever encountering anti-Semites. In New York, you have a choice. Not in Austria."

Austria had to be sued to offer restitution. Refugees from Germany did much better than Austrians. As a matter of fact, the German government invited some of our Shanghai neighbors to come back to Berlin, completely free of charge. Paid the airfare, treated them royally. Austria did nothing of the sort. They made it the most inconvenient process possible, filling out forms every month to prove I was still alive. Deborah refused to do it. She said, "There's no

way in this world I'm putting up with this." I told her, "You're out
of your mind." It wasn't a lot of money, but "Why would you give
them anything?" Even if it only came to $300 a month. She said,
"Like hell I'm going to sit every month and go through this whole
procedure to prove I'm still alive. I don't want it." She had a hard
time telling them to shove it. She must have called three times to tell
them she didn't want their money, to get her off that list. She finally
had to call Vienna and speak to someone at the consulate. She told
them, "You'd better give me the right person this time, I'm sick of
this." They finally dropped her off the list. I think she should have
taken the money.

Most of our friends who were German got quite a bit of restitution. We ex-Austrians were offered a lump sum only if we could
prove what my parents had to leave behind in Austria. They asked
for lists of material things such as jewelry or art, and then we had
to calculate the worth of Papa's business. We also knew that Mutti's
family had to abandon a soda factory somewhere in Poland. Somehow, we had to prove that all these things had been stolen and not
sold. We were children when we left. What did we remember? And
the Nazis certainly hadn't provided us with a bill of sale. The Austrian response was "If you can prove it, prove it."

We attempted to gather documents proving their existence, proving my existence, proving that Mutti's family had really owned a
soda factory, proving, proving, and proving. The one thing I knew
for sure is that Papa had lost his sewing machine. When we finally
accumulated all the paperwork, they paid us what they felt it was
worth. A lump sum of $8,000. For the years and years, my parents
had lived and worked and contributed to the Austrian economy. It
was insulting.

Vienna didn't make me happy, but Walter wasn't into happiness.
Happiness wasn't his thing. Happiness was for other people, fools.
I could not comprehend why any Jew would want to live there,
but I thought, maybe, I would have to readjust my prejudices. I did

not. My visit back only reinforced my opinions. I wrote Vienna off entirely. In fact, I wrote off the whole of Eastern Europe. Why go back to a place with bad memories. Why would I ever want to go to the place where they murdered my mentor and friend?

They murdered Charles Jordan.

I found out when in August of 1967, I opened *The New York Times* and saw an article reporting that his body was found floating in the Vltava River in Prague and that the Czech government was saying he'd committed suicide. I knew immediately he'd been murdered. There was no way in the world Charlie would have killed himself. He loved his work and his life.

The paper laid out his bio. He'd been the key figure in the mass migration of Jews to Israel from Europe and the consequent closing of the displaced person camps in Europe. He'd sponsored the development of Malben, an agency to care for the aged, infirmed, and handicapped immigrants in Israel. He'd been named the executive vice chairman of the JDC. He'd conducted missions for the UN high commissioner for refugees and become the chairman for the International Council of Voluntary Agencies (ICVA) and just prior to his death, was involved in dealings related to Palestinian refugees. They called him the Father of the Refugees.

But nobody knew what had really happened to him. I started to hear stories. One of the stories involved the Czech police, another involved the Palestinians. Then I heard the Egyptians took him to their embassy, and supposedly, he was released, and then he was found dead. I heard that he was mistaken for a Mossad agent, the Israeli intelligence agency, but that was never confirmed.

Then a statement surfaced from a man named Josef Frolík, who for seventeen years worked for Czech intelligence and later defected to America. He claimed that Jordan was suspected by the Arabs of being an Israeli spy and that he'd been kidnapped after leaving his hotel to buy cigarettes. He was brought to the Egyptian embassy for interrogation during which he was killed by three Palestinians.

The next morning, his body was thrown into the river. The Czech authorities were aware of his murder, but decided not to inform the American embassy. Three days after the body was found, the first secretary at the Egyptian embassy in Prague left the country at the government's request, and the three Palestinians left a week later. I had no idea if any of that was true, but it was the only report I could find.

I never knew what Charlie really did for his work. I suspected he was involved in sub-rosa activities getting Jews out of the Soviet Union, making deals with the blessings of the State Department or the CIA. He never talked about it. I was always surprised that he could move so freely behind the Iron Curtain, back and forth. He was quite open about the work he did on behalf of refugees, but he never intimated it went any further than that. I never asked direct questions, and he wouldn't have answered anyway. Despite our closeness, he would have lied to me. The truth would have been too dangerous to admit.

His memorial service at Carnegie Hall was standing room only. In the midst of a job that required enormous vision, the scope of which was incomprehensible, Charlie formed intimate bonds and close personal relationships with thousands of refugees, me included. Charlie had believed in me, had supported me, and had opened doors for me. Losing Charlie was like losing both a second father and a best friend in one fell swoop. It was a debt that could not be repaid.

SISTER

Walter's visit to my father's Romanian family had stirred up even more trouble. Papa's niece and her husband wanted to move to the United States and asked if Ed and I would sponsor them for citizenship. I had no choice but to help. Papa had always felt indebted to his brother, and we owed our very lives to their father. But Romania was behind the Iron Curtain, and I had no idea how to get my cousins across the border. The State Department was willing to transport a deceased American citizen out of the country, but they certainly weren't going to help us transport refugees.

Charles Jordan had already been murdered, which had come as such a shock. I'll never forget that phone call from Ilie. It broke his heart to read about it in the paper. They'd been so close. Losing Charlie was like losing his second father. So Ilie stayed in touch with his widow. She gave Ilie the name of a man and literally said, "Don't ask me questions. Just go to this man, he'll be able to tell you what to do." Sure enough, two weeks later, we got a letter saying "Your family is in Paris."

Ed and I flew to Paris and found them in some godforsaken little place. Only there weren't two people, there were nine! Romania was very smart. For the money, they got rid of the two young people we paid for plus, they threw in all the old, sick ones for free. We opened the door to find Papa's brother, who was already sick, his wife, their daughter and son, the retarded brother, and the in-laws, both in their nineties. Romania had been footing all of their medical bills. This was their chance to dump them off. All of a sudden, we were looking at eight people and a pregnant, twenty-year-old chemical engineer. I knew what it was like to be a refugee. I couldn't leave them in Paris. I decided to move them to America to live with us.

We called the Hebrew Immigrant Aid Society, which helps Jewish refugees get out of a country, and the lady told me very clearly, "I wouldn't recommend you do this. Our experience has been, with other people who have brought refugees to America, they're going to want what you have. They're not going to be grateful. They're going to make your life miserable." I thought to myself, "What a horrible thing to say. That won't happen to us."

We were living in New Jersey at the time. Our house had three bedrooms. We added three more bedrooms, two bathrooms, another kitchen, and truckloads of new furniture. I made the salesman's day when I ordered eight new beds. My two sons were wonderful about sharing our home with complete strangers, and Ed was never around to complain or care. He was traveling, working as a consultant for the retail industry and usually only home one week in a month. He was gone so much my youngest son announced he would never be a high-paid executive because he didn't want to do that kind of traveling. Ed was responsible for stores all over the country. He had to do in-person consultations and site visits. It was his job, but it meant we spent most, if not all, of our daily life without him.

Despite a house full of people, I still felt like the lonely new wife I'd been in Texas. Only this time, Ed wasn't flying the planes, he was just on them all the time. He'd become such a frequent flyer that the stewardesses knew his name and to leave him alone and let him sleep. I hated sitting at home. The boys were in school; the Romanians had their own lives. I felt I had to do something, not just be a daytime-TV watcher. I still suffered from the nagging belief that I had no talent, that I was stupid, that I had nothing to contribute to the world. A belief instilled in me by that I.Q. test from my childhood.

I decided to retake the I.Q. test without telling Ed or my boys or anyone else. I was terrified I would score poorly. It had always puzzled me how I could have done so well in school and be considered so slow. I just needed to know on my own. I was relieved when the scores came back. I wasn't a genius, but I wasn't an idiot, either. All those years I'd been so insecure about my intelligence; I'd short-changed myself not only in confidence, but also in my education.

I decided to start taking college courses. Courses and courses and courses. I took so many I could have become a doctor. I studied art, architecture, interior design, languages. I had a love for languages and became even more interested when I saw my Spanish teacher. He was extremely handsome, and I developed quite a crush on him. I didn't know the feeling was mutual.

Then one night, I was on the train heading home from visiting Ilie in the city when I ran into him. He was teaching night classes at Columbia, and he gave me his schedule. I found myself visiting my brother more often, which allowed me to "run into" the teacher again and again. I would sit next to him, blushing and nervous. Finally, I confided in one of my friends. She had already had an affair, so she was the only one I could tell "I have a crush on my teacher." She offered to drive me to the station so I wouldn't have a way home. He'd have to give me a ride. If he wasn't on the train, I could call her, and she'd pick me up. It was her plan, but I went along with it.

I met my brother for dinner in the city and kept a close eye on my watch. I had to be on that train. I took my usual seat, and at first, I didn't see my teacher. Then there he was. He sat next to me, and we chatted. I mentioned casually that a friend had dropped me at the station. He offered me a ride home.

We pulled in front of my house and talked a bit more. I didn't want to get out of the car, but I was a married woman even if my husband was never even in the same state three weeks out of every month. There was a strong attraction that could have blossomed had I been more reckless, but I wasn't a reckless woman, much to my dismay. I got out of the car and returned to my family. It's the closest I ever came to cheating.

It wasn't because I was unhappy. I was, in fact, the happiest I had ever been in my life. I had always wanted a big extended family around me with aunts and uncles and kids and cousins, and now, I finally had it. Our house bustled with activity, twelve people coming and going, and I didn't mind at all. I really didn't. The Romanians ate their big meal in the afternoon, and we ate ours at night. We had a routine, and my aunt was a great cook. She would bake extra goodies and leave them for us. I never had to worry about cleaning. They were immaculate. In fact, they were so clean, when my aunt did all the cooking, she wore a kerchief around her hair.

Of course, food shopping broke the bank every week. We'd fill four grocery carts. They didn't realize that whatever they put in the carts cost money. They thought it was all free, and they kept piling on stuff. I would have kept taking care of them until we ran out of money altogether. I just kept spending money and kept myself ignorant, figuring Ed would let me know when it was time to stop. I took the affidavit of support I signed on their behalf quite literally. It said to be responsible as sponsors, so I made sure we were responsible for every cent.

Then my uncle's heart condition put him into the hospital, and the pregnant cousin had her baby. We were crippled with medical bills. I begged the doctors to treat them for free to no avail. The hospital would not even release the baby to our care until we paid them in full. I was running our finances into the ground on their behalf. Somehow, Ed found the money, and we paid the bill, but there was no more room at the inn. Mark and Mitch had to give up their room to accommodate the newborn. They loved having a baby in the house. They'd swaddle the baby so tightly the infant could have stood up straight.

Ed was working nonstop supporting twelve people. Once the baby was born, it became clear the two youngest Romanians needed to get to work. They were chemical engineers, and they spoke English, so Ed was able, thanks to his connections, to secure jobs for them. We breathed a sigh of relief. Maybe now, they would be able to support themselves. Maybe now, the medical bills would be paid. That's when greed finally reared its ugly head.

After the younger ones had been working for a while, they said, "We want to take a driving test so we can drive to work."

Ed said, "Sure, we'll pay for the driving test." Then we decided to buy them a used car. No, they didn't want a used car.

They said, "No, we were told a used car is dangerous. We need a new car."

That's when Ed had it. He said, "I'm not giving you a bad car. I'm just buying you a used car."

To which they responded, "When are you buying us a house like yours?"

Ed turned to me and said, "I want them out. Now."

We rented them three apartments, completely furnished, and hired movers to help with the relocation. The Romanians were furious. They wouldn't speak to us. They felt we owed them. After a year of entirely supporting them, I still felt guilty. Mutti loved them so dearly I felt she would be angry with me for putting them out.

I tried to explain, "Look, we have to work for what we have." I explained we had struggled, scrimped, and saved to be able to afford a home. Even though Ed's parents had money, he wanted to be his own man. Because he didn't want to ever owe anybody anything, he never took a dime. He was proud of being self-made.

They didn't care. It was mostly the young people who spoke to me with hostility, but it didn't matter—the old ones must have agreed. So they left and wouldn't talk to us again. It was a hard and expensive lesson for me to learn, to accept that I could never go back and rescue myself as a refugee. No amount of generosity toward another family member could save me from my childhood. It did not ease the ache. It did not fill the void in my heart. Mutti and Papa were gone. They could never be replaced. I probably should have moved the Romanians into apartments in the first place.

BROTHER

It was through Mrs. Jordan, Charlie's wife, that we found a man to get Papa's family out of Romania. The man lived in Queens. He said, "It's going to cost $10,000 in cash."

I had a wealthy cousin who was in real estate, and with his resources plus the help of several other family members, we got the cash together. I made an appointment to see the man. My lawyer cousin and I took the subway out toward Astoria, in the middle of the night, rain pouring down. I carried the bills in a little paper bag. I thought for certain the bag would disintegrate in my hands.

We wound up in a small apartment building on the second floor. We rang the bell. A woman answered and said, "Wait here." So we waited in the living room with other people. Nobody looked at each other. We waited and waited and waited. Finally, a short man came out and said, "Come into my office." We followed him as he took his place behind his desk.

I asked him, "How do you carry the cash back and forth to Romania?"

He said, "In my pocket."

I said, "Isn't anybody looking?"

He said, "Who looks?"

Apparently, the Romanian government and the American government were aware of his business, so we gave him the money. My cousin, the lawyer, had drawn a contract for the man to sign. "Would you mind signing?" we asked.

The man shrugged, aloof. "Sure, not at all!"

He took the money, put it in his pocket, and signed the document without so much as a glance at what he was signing. I thought to myself, "There goes ten grand." But what could we do? We had to try.

He said, "I'll be in touch."

I waited a month before I called him to ask, "What's happening?"

He said, "I will call you when the time is ready."

Three months later, I got a phone call, "Your family will be in Paris tomorrow." And they were.

Deborah and Ed bought plane tickets and flew over to meet them. Deborah was shocked by their living conditions and called me to say that the Romanians felt they had been ill treated by the man we'd paid to get them out. They'd been forced to sell all their belongings to him for almost nothing. He was making money on both sides apparently. Certainly, he had to bribe people, and bribes were expensive, but he also had quite a business going for himself. The Romanians were left penniless and stranded. Deborah decided to take them in. She was much more generous than I cared to be, and Ed wouldn't say no. Ed knew the whole story of how they had saved our lives in Vienna. He knew we owed them. Plus Deborah was right; it was the human thing to do.

They came from a culture where they had to take advantage to get ahead, in order to survive. In Romania, if you don't take advantage, you won't have a job, you won't have money, and you will have nothing. Everybody outside the family is a potential enemy and even inside the family, who knows? They were wired into that. They brought it with them. They got to America, they saw Ed's home, and they assumed he was wealthy. He had a car and a house, and he was working as a consultant at the time that meant he was traveling constantly. They felt, "He should take care of us." Deborah called me and told me they wanted a new car and a house. I told her, "You've done enough!" It caused bad blood. We lost touch. Such is life.

While Deborah was busy adopting, feeding, and clothing the Romanians, Sylvia and I had added to our own family, having our second daughter, Darin. I'd become the head designer at Originala. I was known. I didn't have my name on the label, which irked me, but I got my name in *Vogue*, in *Harper's*: "Ilie Wacs for Originala." I was always in the press even if Originala wouldn't put me on the label.

I'd been working for them for eight years when I was contacted by a conglomerate that had a cheap apparel business that was losing money. They had great facilities, and they thought if they got a name designer, they could turn their business around. They showed me their warehouses in New Jersey. You could have parked 747 jet planes in there, and they would have gotten lost. They had a production capacity for tens of thousands of garments. I made garments in the hundreds. Even though it made no sense to hire me, they made me an offer I couldn't refuse. They were putting my name on the label. I told Sylvia, "We'll see what happens." I left Originala and took two of their officers with me, one of them the son-in-law of Originala. They were very hurt. They offered to put my name on the door, to put my name on the label, but it was too late. I wanted to be on my own. We formed Ilie Wacs, Inc.

My partners were supposed to take care of the sales, production, and whatnot. Business wasn't doing great. The conglomerate was used to projections. In the haute-couture business, you couldn't give projections. You had no idea what you were going to sell three months in advance, but they needed numbers, so we made them up. My production manager wanted to show we were cutting costs, so he kept cutting coats to bring down the cost of each garment's production. Meanwhile, we were up to our neck in coats. The chickens came home to roost eventually.

Toward the end of the first year, I went to a show in Florida at Neiman Marcus, and my partners came along to play golf. There was no one in the showroom to take care of customers. One of the owners from the conglomerate walked in, and the receptionist stopped him, "May I ask who you are, sir?" He was the kind of Irishman who could turn instantly red in the face. On command, he yelled, "Where is everybody?" She said, "In Florida," and he yelled, "This is not a business. This is a fucking boutique!" And that was the end of Ilie Wacs, Inc. I came back from Florida, and the conglomerate walked away from the entire business. My partners did too.

I had a good location on Seventh Avenue. The landlord came to me and said, "Why don't you just keep doing it yourself?" I said "I can't do it myself." He said, "I tell you what I'll do. I'll give you six months free rent." The conglomerate had walked away from the equipment and left me with all of the production facilities. It seemed stupid not to give it a try. With my friend, Werner, we pitched in some money and got started.

Sylvia took over the bookkeeping, and she became the brains of the business. She had a head for numbers that allowed me to just focus on designing. She took care of everything in our lives and pushed me to achieve and acquire far more than I would have on my own. She found an apartment on Central Park West overlooking the reservoir. She wanted to buy it, but I was too chicken. Our business was barely two years old, and we had a rent-controlled brownstone that was fine for me. Even our accountant called me and said, "I speak to you like an uncle. Don't do it!" I handed Sylvia the phone, and she listened to him carefully, hung up, and announced, "Now I'm for sure buying that apartment."

She bought land in Long Island and insisted we build a summer home on a cliff overlooking the beach. It was spectacular—all glass. There was one main house with a deck wrapped all around with a beautiful view of the ocean. We were right on top of a rock. There was a little bridge that led to my studio where I could paint. Everything was built in. Everything. Even the bedrooms. It was all clean with the beams showing. It was simple. Everything was natural, except for the upholstery, which was white. The kitchen was white except for the cabinets. It was isolated. There were no neighbors. Nothing. I sat on the lounge chair all night long, listening to the ocean. I painted. It was a great gift to us, that house.

Sylvia could buy two buildings in an afternoon without me hearing a word about it. She could make a decision that fast. I never even wrote a check for our rent. I had no idea what our rent even was! She was the take-charge person, and that never bothered me. My ego was never involved. I knew she did it better than I could do it, so we never had a conflict about it. I just wanted to design. There was a clear line for us. Business ended at five o'clock. It was separate from our personal life. It was a job. At home, we discussed the children, their schools, politics, and theater.

In the fashion business, you start from scratch every season. You're only as hot as your current show. There is absolutely no memory in the business. The stores want new, but not too new. The press wants something they can splash across their magazines. By the time the shows arrive, you're ready to shoot yourself. You can't try to please anyone but yourself. I learned to go by instinct, and I did what I liked. Everybody else could take it or leave it.

I liked that the industry was dog eat dog. There was no pretense about it. Nobody pretended to be gentlemanly or following a higher calling. Mills tried to sell you shoddy stuff, buyers made unreasonable demands, someone would try to pass off the wrong fabric, and you just learned to say "no" as loudly and as forcefully as you could.

Buyers would tell me, "People don't buy fitted coats. People won't wear color." They wanted dumb coats. We called them "bagels," which was Seventh Avenue lingo for a dumb coat. They wanted bagels with plain silhouettes, straight up and down. No way I would make a bagel and put my name on it. I made fitted coats with color, and surprise, surprise, everyone loved them. I became the Coat King of Seventh Avenue.

I enjoyed the spectacle of the shows, I did. I liked to do my own running commentary, little asides and whatnot. It would take two months to put together a collection of eighty or ninety pieces, and out of those, I'd only show fifty-five or sixty. Putting together a collection required a balancing act. In order to pay the rent, I had to design coats that appealed to customers, but those were not the coats that generated press. Magazine editors were looking for the offbeat, the next big thing, a vision, a style. Wearability was not their concern. It was a conundrum. You couldn't sell to the former without the publicity of the latter. I wound up designing two collections, one for buyers and one for press.

I did very well with *Vogue*. Diana Vreeland liked what I did a lot. She looked like a strange bird. White skin with pitch-black hair, she resembled a kabuki actress, always dressed in black. Her office walls were bright red, shiny lacquer red. She knew exactly what she liked and disliked. She was always accompanied by Nicolas de Gainsbourg. He was the fashion editor and a former Ballets Russes dancer. He looked the part. Elegant and always with a white shirt and black tie.

Most of the time, they came to the collection and picked pieces from the runway, but once in a while, Ms. Vreeland would get a bee in her bonnet, and she'd call wanting me to make her a very specific piece. She'd be rather vague about her specifications. At one point, she called saying she needed "a nice white summer suit. You have something?" What, was I going to say, no? When Diana Vreeland called, you jumped to it. A spread in *Vogue* was free publicity. "Can I have it tomorrow?" She needed everything instantly. Yesterday. "Yes, of course." I quickly dropped everything else and started making the white suit. I didn't have any fabric, so I cut the suit in muslin. I went to her office with my model and showed it to her. She said, "I love the fabric! Don't you?" and everyone said, "Yes, yes, we love it!" I never said a word. I wasn't going to tell her it was muslin.

Once the suit hit her pages, I had to have a store credit. Saks bought two or three pieces just to be able to get the free publicity. They knew that what she liked wouldn't sell, nobody would want it, but these weren't paid ads, these were editorial ads making it extremely valuable to Saks. They ordered a few, which we made in the sample room, and nobody made money on that. If somebody had walked into a Saks asking for the suit, we would have been in real trouble. To see my designs in the pages of *Vogue*, to see my name on those pages, my heart twisted with the slightest sadness. Papa never got to see my success. It was my biggest regret.

SISTER

I was in the audience for Ilie's first show at the Plaza Hotel in New York. The major press and celebrities were seated in front of me. Betty Furness and Bernadine Morris, the fashion editor of *The New York Times*; Eugenia Sheppard, the top writer for the *Herald Tribune*; and beside her was then-supermodel Lauren Hutton. The lights dimmed, and the music began to play, and I could barely breathe, I was so excited for him.

The models came down the runway and how they walked, how they carried themselves. Ilie wasn't one to care about the face, he'd say, "Just watch them on the runway, see how gorgeous they become." It was true. You couldn't take your eyes off of the girls as they marched by in coats and suits. For the finale, he had a stunning African-American model come out in a long red evening gown. It was a very tight-fitting simple silk sheath with tight sleeves and a slit all the way to her thigh. It was about as sexy as you can get. There was a dramatic hood draped around her face. Then, in the middle of the walk, she slipped the hood off her head and onto her shoulders, and it became a cape.

People went wild. They were standing and applauding, and Ilie wouldn't come out. He stayed in the back, and finally, the models had to drag him out. One was behind pushing him and two were on either side dragging him. He didn't need that kind of attention. He was just happy they loved it. He didn't feel he had to take a bow, but the applause was deafening. He wouldn't go any further than the runway entrance. He just waved and went back in. I thought to myself, "My God, Mutti and Papa didn't live to see it. This is what they worked for. This is what they hoped for. This is what they prayed for. How unfair is it that they can't be here to see it?"

They had always been so proud of my brother. They bragged about him all the time. I did, too. Ilie was so talented from such an early age that we basked in his glory. He was the favorite son, but it didn't bother me one bit. I wasn't jealous of him, ever. If he won an award, I couldn't wait to tell everyone. I was his biggest cheerleader. Sometimes, talent is so obvious, it becomes truth, and I'd never felt that was more truthful than on his big night at the Plaza.

BROTHER

Sylvia was diagnosed with breast cancer, and her doctor wanted her to have a mastectomy. Sylvia, being the strong, sometimes stubborn woman that she was, she didn't want to hear about a mastectomy. So she went to another doctor who advised her just to have a lumpectomy. She felt the survival rate was comparable, and she didn't want the disfigurement of a full mastectomy. She spent three weeks in the hospital where they implanted a radioactive isotope inside her, and I couldn't go near her. That was supposed to have taken care of it.

She was fine for almost two years, working all the time. Then they began to see spots in other places, in the bone, in the lymph nodes, and then the brain. There were disputed opinions about whether or not it was preexistent. One doctor was very negative about it. Another would say, "It's not in the bone." You tend to seek out medical advice that tells you what you want to hear. You can always find that. Fake doctors and whatnot. We listened to the more optimistic of the two.

She started having trouble walking and was having back pains, but we thought it was arthritis. We went to Galisteo, New Mexico, on the recommendation of her friend who believed in holistic, alternative medicine. There was a healer who was involved with Shirley MacLaine. I was not going to discourage her. I didn't believe in it, but I felt if it would make her happy, that would be a good thing.

So we went to the New Mexico healer. Sylvia wasn't feeling well at all. She couldn't walk off the airplane. I got a wheelchair for her. When we arrived at the compound, the healer passed her hand over Sylvia and said, "You don't have cancer. You're fine." I said, "Well, medical opinion says otherwise." She gave us a vague answer.

When we landed back in New York, I had to take Sylvia directly to the hospital. Maris had just met the man she was going to marry, and he came to meet Sylvia at her bedside. He was a nice-looking man, and Sylvia was happy to meet him. Though the marriage did not last, I was glad Sylvia had the chance to connect with Maris on that day. They hadn't always seen eye to eye. Mothers and daughters, it's complicated.

Sylvia never made it out of that hospital. It wasn't a surprise. The girls were devastated. It was a terrible blow to us all. Despite knowing it was going to happen, it was still a shock. There is just no way to prepare yourself for the inevitable.

It was difficult to run the business without Sylvia. The people I hired to replace her weren't nearly half as competent. I had to relearn every aspect of what she covered. I had to transform myself into a businessman. I didn't have her input, her judgment to rely on. It was very hard to make decisions without her. She'd been doing the job of three or four people without breaking a sweat. She was irreplaceable.

The business went on, and I became financially successful instead of just a critical darling. We'd struggled while Sylvia was alive, and I wished she'd had a chance to see it bloom. I thought about her often and regretted certain moments. I could have been more attentive to her. I was busy with work. It was always what I wanted to do, not so much what she wanted to do. I could have been a better husband. I would have stayed with Sylvia for the rest of my life. We had a good marriage. We argued. We laughed. We built a wonderful life with each other. She was very hard to lose. It took me a year to feel like myself. I was very clear I never wanted to marry again. I had no intention of taking on another family. I was happy with the one I had. I didn't need a house full of Romanians like Deborah. Plus, my heart wasn't into dating. It was better to be alone.

Then, two years after Sylvia died, I met Susan. I had just started dating a lady who was hosting a small birthday party for a friend. She had a civil relationship with her ex-husband and invited him to attend. He arrived with Susan, a lawyer, as his date. I liked her immediately. She had two daughters the exact same age as my daughters and was active with child-adoption law, smart, very smart. Eventually, the lady and I broke up, then Susan and the ex-husband broke up, and we switched.

We began talking every night, then spending our weekends and summers together, but I really meant it when I said I would never marry again. Fortunately, Susan felt the same way. She had no desire to remarry. She kept her apartment, and I kept mine. On Sundays, we both went home. It was the perfect arrangement for us both, and it has seen us through more than twenty years.

SISTER

With Ed's constantly evolving consulting opportunities and with Mutti no longer two doors down, we moved from New Jersey to Washington, D.C. Because Ed was still traveling three weeks out of every month, I got busy using the numerous degrees I'd accumulated through my coursework. I opened the design center for Bloomingdales and had a wonderful boss who allowed me to really shine and take credit for my own work. With Ed out of state for our opening, I had to bask in my own glory, unescorted. In D.C., I was extremely well respected, had a great reputation as a designer, and I liked the attention. Gone were the days when an I.Q. test could keep me in the corner. I loved my job. I was finally coming into my own. I wasn't happy in the slightest when Ed said we were moving to San Francisco.

Ed had been working as a consultant for a company called the Gap, and their president, Don Fisher, had become quite impressed with him. He wanted Ed to turn a mail-order catalog called Banana Republic into a series of retail stores. At first, Ed said no. He wasn't interested, but Don wouldn't take no for an answer. He persisted, and Ed finally said yes. We were going to have to move again.

I didn't have a say in it anymore than I had as a kid being toted from Vienna to Shanghai to New York to Canada and back again. As a designer, I was assertive, but once I came home, I retreated back into my shell. I let my husband speak for me. He was extremely bright, highly competitive, though not with me because he didn't consider me competition. I was afraid to bloom in front of him. He used to joke and say he got the best of both worlds. He married a Jewish woman with an Asian background. A white woman who would walk behind him ten paces. He had no idea I was a Sleeping Tiger.

But Ed was a good provider, a straight arrow, and he'd do anything for me. He indulged my every whim. If I felt the whole house needed new furniture, we got new furniture. If I wanted jewelry, I got jewelry. There wasn't a thing he wouldn't do for me because he understood, probably even better than I did at the time, that my insatiable need for material possessions originated in that childhood of depravation. That need reached its peak once we moved to San Francisco.

We bought a house with a pool, and finally, I thought, all those dreams I had dreamed while in Shanghai hiding behind the flowered curtain were coming true. Finally, the incessant sense of constant wanting would go away now that I had my own pool and even help around the house, with gardeners, cooks, and cleaning ladies coming and going. San Francisco was Shangri-la. So why was I still restless? I had no sense of fulfillment. I thought maybe expanding the house would help. I made it into a two story. I added a deck and a hot tub. Still, it wasn't enough. I just kept wanting, wanting, wanting. When Ed went on a business trip, I went on a house tour with an agent.

She was the agent who sold us our first house. We were meeting for lunch, socially. I wasn't in the market. She called to cancel our lunch because she had to go to two open houses. I agreed to tag along in order to keep our date. These were open houses for agents, not for buyers. She told me, "You can't say anything because if they find out you're not an agent, I'm going to get in trouble."

I walked through the first house, and I wanted it. My agent thought I was kidding. I wasn't. It didn't have a pool. It just had a big piece of land. It had a pond. It had a hot tub in the bedroom. It had a lot of little rooms, but there was something about it and something about the area. It was on flat land. We were living always on hills.

I told her I'd like to make an offer and that I didn't want to start lower because I didn't want to lose it. She was shocked with me. "What about Ed? What's he going to say?" I told her to make the offer contingent upon his approval. I put down a deposit to show I was serious. I wrote that little check out of my checking account, and I didn't even know if I had the funds to cover it. Ed called that night, and I told him "I just saw the perfect house. I'd love to buy it."

He said, "I didn't know we were looking for houses."

I said, "Ed, I just made an offer." He actually hung up on me.

I knew he was coming home two days later. I figured when he got back, we would discuss it. Later that evening, I heard the garage door opening. Ed had hopped the next flight back to San Francisco. He yelled at me, "What the fuck did you do!"

I sputtered, "It's the most gorgeous house!"

I tried to convince him it was perfect, that the area was perfect, I had to have it. He calmed down a bit.

Then he asked me, "What did they ask?"

I told him what my offer was, and he said, "No, I meant what were they asking?"

I said, "That's what they were asking."

He took a deep breath. "That's not an offer. You gave them what they asked for."

I said, "Yes."

He was yelling again. "You'd think you'd have enough sense to offer less!" He was upset with me to say the least.

I took him to see the house the next day. He went with the intention of saying no. I was double-talking. I knew the house needed work, but I kept those thoughts in my own head. Ed seemed incredulous. "You like all this? Compared to what you just did in the other house, you think this is really good?"

I said, "I would definitely want to change the windows."

He saw all the rooms, then he saw the pond. He said "A fish pond? Who's going to take care of the fish?"

I said, "Well, we don't have to keep that. We could put a pool in."

He said, "A what?"

We went outside. I hadn't realized that we had two acres, which was quite a bit for Hillsborough; the majority of people had half an acre, maybe an acre. The house behind us had five acres. Well, I didn't see the house, I just saw the lawn. I told Ed, "This is all ours," which wasn't true. Our two acres went the other direction. I just saw all the green, and I said to Ed, "Look at all this land. We don't have all that land in the other house."

His tone changed. He was impressed now. "All this? Really?" I just kept talking and talking, and he finally said, "Well, I guess we're buying it, aren't we?"

Ed had patience with me because he understood my restlessness. Though we never had conversations about my childhood, he knew I wouldn't discuss it, he always kept it in mind when dealing with me. He'd tell Ilie, "You know Deborah—she's still making up for what she didn't have." I could never have enough to compensate for what happened in China. It seemed impossible to me. For other people, they came to peace with those years, but I couldn't. Ilie wasn't needy at all. If he had a little room with a stool, he would have been happy. Those years in Vienna had trained him to need only one thing from life: freedom. Me, I just kept spending money, thinking it would miraculously stop the need. It never filled that gaping hole. It couldn't fix the past.

Ed knew me. He got it. He indulged me. He respected me more because I'd had a tough background. He liked that I hadn't grown up privileged. I just hated that every time we met someone new, he'd launch right into my whole story. Like the time we were seated beside Count Chandon and his wife at a gala. I heard Ed saying, "The minute I met her, I was in love with her. I knew right away. Whoever would think this little gal from China, blah, blah, blah." I could have taken the bread knife and opened his throat, I was so mad. To make matters worse, he gave dates! So not only did he tell them I was from China, he told them how old I was! I could never get him to understand that I was ashamed of my childhood even though it was completely out of my control.

Ed was an open book. About himself, he had no problem telling people he went to Brooklyn College, that he "paid for it myself!" He could have gone to Boston University. He could have gone to Syracuse. He didn't want to. Brooklyn College was convenient, didn't cost much money, he didn't want his parents paying for it. They could have paid for it several times over. He wanted his independence. The people we dealt with, in his job and socially, they were born with silver spoons in their mouths. They went to Harvard, Princeton, or to Yale. It was a given. I never found it necessary for him to explain where he went to college. Nobody asked him. He volunteered it! He was proud, and he wanted me to stop being embarrassed about my past. I didn't want the past to catch up with me. The past was the past, leave it alone.

So I called the contractor I used to work with and tried to build my future. We walked through the whole house, and at the end of our tour, he told me, "You're better off just getting rid of the house completely. Just leave the garage to make it look like a remodel so you won't be paying taxes." I absolutely could not tell Ed, but there was no way I could just paint and move in. I had to gradually break the news.

First, I showed him plans of what it could look like, and he didn't for a second realize this was a whole new house. He questioned me, "That inside looks elaborate, and it's rather large . . . where is that space coming from?"

I said, "We're taking away all the other walls, and we're going further back." I was lying to him, basically. I showed him more drawings and excused the changes by saying they were on a quarter-inch scale, that it "looks big, but it really isn't as big as it looks. I mean, if you took down all these walls, you'd understand it, but you really don't understand architecture like I do."

But Ed wasn't stupid. He said, "Look at it, Deborah! This has enormous doors that go up God knows how high. It doesn't make sense!"

I tried to disguise the fact that the old house would be replaced by a new one. I skipped over the details and said I was extremely excited. "I can't wait to move, it's so wonderful! It's going to be perfect, and Ed, you always travel, but you know me, I need to have a beautiful home, blah, blah, blah." Then I admitted, "It's really a brand new house. We have to get rid of this one."

Oh my God. He actually walked out of the house. I didn't see him for hours and hours. He checked into a hotel and stayed overnight. He came home the next day and said, "Just don't talk to me."

During this time, we'd actually sold the house in which we lived. It was going to take at least a year to build the new home, and the people who bought our house had no intention of waiting a year to move in. They wanted to be in within thirty days. We lived out of boxes in an apartment for over a year. I went every day and watched construction. I had to make sure they did it exactly to the specifications. I could do the drawings, but since I wasn't an architect, I couldn't sign off. Every nook and cranny I designed. After a while, Ed got used to it, and as he kept going there, he could see the way it advanced, and he actually got a kick out of it. We still had plenty of arguments. We needed to rip out the existing lawn because the sprinkler system wasn't any good. Then, we were in the middle of a drought, and Ed thought it was stupid to build a pool if we couldn't put water in it. I suggested we get a cover made, and he said he'd never heard of anything as stupid as that. I found a place in San Jose that would deliver water and had huge trucks come in to fill the pool. Then Ed complained about all that grass in the middle of a drought. I had the great idea—you don't ever want to worry about planting? Put a tennis court in!

Ed said, "That's an expensive way to worry about not watering."

I said, "Mitchell loves to play tennis." I put it on my son, who was at that point a tournament player. Believe me, he didn't need his own tennis court.

One thing led to another to another to another—by the time we were done Ed said, "We'll never be able to move out of here. Nobody's ever going to be able to figure out how much this is worth because there's nothing to compare it to."

There was nothing not to love. I built it. I made it my dream house, built it to house all our artwork. I built it like a gallery. My living room was an art gallery where around the perimeter hung all the art with five feet of space to walk. In the middle, I created the feeling of a courtyard. The ceiling was forty-eight-feet high. The room was forty-five feet by sixty-eight feet. Even the contractor said to me, it's too big a space for a living room. It's like a bowling alley. I wanted it that big. You live in one room, on top of your entire family for the whole of your childhood, you want space. Lots and lots of space.

Because we didn't have a bathroom as a child, I designed eight bathrooms. Every room had to have its own bathroom. Even the family room had to have a guest bath. That obviously had a lot to do with China, the conditions in which I lived and bathed all those years. My parents would have been elated. They would have thought they died and went to heaven. I finally found my home. I felt I had finally escaped my past.

A totally different person emerged from somewhere deep within me. I started fundraising, planning huge, star-studded galas for medical research, dinners for diseases, each event growing grander in scale. I'd seen rampant disease in the ghetto of Shanghai. I'd been surrounded by it daily. Maybe that was why most of my energy and my efforts were directed toward medical research. There were enormous risks with each event. Organizations would trust me with half-a-million dollars in seed money, and there was always the possibility that we'd raise nothing. If I couldn't raise a minimum of a million dollars, the event was useless. Then there were the diseases themselves, some were controversial, like the fundraiser I did for stem-cell research where people sent me letters saying I was killing babies. But some of the diseases, like AIDS, were considered taboo, much too dangerous. When I produced the very first AIDS fundraiser held in San Francisco, people actually warned me not to shake patients' hands. A man even said to me, "Come back to me in seven years when you're sick." People were terrified. They wanted me to shut the event down entirely. There were threats from City Hall. People sent me letters saying I was encouraging HIV-positive people to move to San Francisco. There were death threats and prank calls. And it just made me more determined.

No matter the disease, they all required massive education and awareness campaigns that were always, ultimately, overshadowed by the celebrity talent. People didn't want a lecture on stem-cell research or AIDS or brain tumors. They wanted to see Burt Reynolds or Bernadette Peters or Michael Douglas or Jennifer Hudson.

I had to find the guts to call the agents of celebrities and convince them to get involved. There was no use asking them to donate their time. Very few celebrities will show up for free, no matter the cause. I found a determination I never really knew I had, and I liked it. It was the closest I'd ever come to being part of the movies. Producing the events, hiring celebrities, I was finally part of show business. Whatever the reason, it brought me joy, and for the first time in my life, I was scared to death, but doing it anyway. And I was good at it.

So I just kept going. I wanted to see what else I could do. Maybe I could tackle cancer. Maybe I could tackle childhood obesity. Maybe I could go back to Shanghai and look my past in the eye. Maybe I had that strength now. Maybe it was time.

BROTHER

There was a huge change in Deborah when she started fundraising. It built her self-confidence, and she wasn't blending into the woodwork anymore. She had always been a very competent person, but she'd never expressed that side of her personality. Now, she was a walking contradiction. Painfully shy, yet she was doing great things that took great courage.

I went to every one of her events. They were fun. I enjoy the tummel, the whole spectacle, the preparations, the coming and the going, the noise of it. I liked seeing her stand in the limelight. I was amazed by her transformation. There were always problems dealing with the personalities and the performers, the egos and the donors. She was never rattled by it. She was quite regal, elegant. She handled matters with tact and grace. I would have had sleepless nights!

Her husband, Ed, was also shocked by her transformation. He was now the CEO of Banana Republic, both of us were in the schmatte business, though his business was a much bigger business than mine. He was overseeing the expansion of Banana Republic into five hundred stores, securing locations, hiring management. He was quite ruthless. He expected a great deal from people, as much as he expected from himself. He was a hard worker and had always been the star of the show, so we were both surprised when Deborah began to shine on her own. We were even more surprised when she agreed to go to China. She'd kept our childhood in Shanghai a secret from her San Francisco and Peninsula friends. She hated when I spoke of those years and wanted nothing to do with our past. So when Ed was sent to China by Banana Republic and he asked me to join them for the trip, I was floored that Deborah willingly packed her bags. I thought for sure she'd stay home.

P_{ART} V

SHANGHAI

BROTHER

Because of Ed's company, we got the royal treatment all over the country. We were issued an official guide and saw everything in China we'd never been able to see as children. When we arrived in Shanghai, I told the guide, "I'm going to be the guide tomorrow. I'll show you where to go." He drove us to Hongkou where the ghetto used to be, and I told him "Do you know where Chusan Road is?" He wasn't quite sure, so we drove around, then I remembered. "There used to be a big jail here. Is the jail still there?"

He happily said, "Yes!"

"Just left of the jail, park there." I knew where to walk from there.

Our old apartment was still standing. We climbed the stairs to see the room, and it was remarkable, nothing had changed. Deborah even claimed it was the same wallpaper. In 1944 during the war, I'd made a drawing from the window of the room facing the street, and looking out from that same window, I took a photograph. It was the exact same view. Forty-four years later, nothing had changed.

I felt I had stepped into a time warp. I took a walk by myself and half expected Walter to join me or for the White Russians to jump out from behind a building to chase us down the street. It was the weirdest feeling. Everything looked the same, only I had changed. The streets were the same. People looked the same. It was really a very disconcerting feeling. Before I went, I made an effort to study a little Chinese because I always felt bad about not having become fluent. How could I have lived for so many years in that country and not adapted to the native tongue? Miraculously, I remembered a few words, and when I spoke, the dialect came right back. The locals got a big kick out of me. A white-haired, Jewish American speaking Chinese with a Shanghai dialect jogging through the streets for exercise. Forty odd years later, I was still turning heads.

SISTER

Ed felt it was important for Mark and Mitchell to see where I'd grown up, but my older son, Mark, had a girlfriend he didn't want to leave, which is why we asked Ilie to join us instead. We hadn't been back since we were children. I wasn't crazy about the idea, but forty years had passed, so I begrudgingly joined the expedition.

It was the most amazing experience. We went to Shanghai, Beijing, and Hong Kong over the course of ten days. When we saw the Terra Cotta Soldiers in Xian, it started raining. The air was so dirty, it rained mud. I got sick. I couldn't breathe. We toured a farm later that day, and the farmer offered to give me acupuncture. I wasn't brave enough to accept his generosity, so I waited until we got to Hong Kong. I kept going. As soon as we got to Hong Kong, the hotel sent a doctor and nurse to my room. They were both wearing uniforms. The doctor injected me with something, and the next day, I was perfect. We could sightsee again.

Ilie kept a drawing pad with him the entire time. We went to see Mao's tomb. Mao was encased in glass, and when we walked out into Tiananmen Square, there was a big picture of him hanging. Ilie decided to sketch Mao, and as he drew, more and more Chinese lined up behind him to see. At some point, there were as many people circled around Ilie as there were in line to go into the tomb. When Ed looked at the drawing he told Ilie, "Quickly, do something else," because Ilie was drawing Mao exactly the way he looked, but he resembled Mickey Mouse. Mao had a big head and big ears. Ilie's sketch started from the outside in with those big ears. People around us were appalled. Quickly, Ed told him "Stop sketching, or make something out of it because they're not going to be happy." Ilie redid it.

Ilie and my youngest son, Mitchell, were rooming together. They had a ball because they were both fearless. Ed and I were too anxious to go out at night and experiment and eat from the street vendors. Ilie didn't think twice about it. He did his daily morning jog whether he knew the area or not. Everywhere we went, he enjoyed himself. He had no problem picking up the language again. He was able to remember it.

I saw more in those ten days than I ever saw while I lived there. As a kid, I was never allowed to travel outside the district. I spent ten-and-a-half years within a few block radius. With my return, I developed a stronger appreciation for the culture. I could finally see it from a different point of view. I wasn't living there anymore. We were not staying in the same conditions, and I had no emotional connection to the places we visited because I'd never seen them before. I didn't become emotional until we went back to Chusan Road.

When we got to the ghetto, we stood out like sore thumbs. We were the only non-Chinese people on the streets. It was not a well-traveled sightseeing area. It was a pathetic, poor place where a tourist bus would never go. The fact we were even standing there was cause for curiosity. We came with a car and a driver that drew even more attention, and then Ilie started sketching. The children chased after him. There were "Oohs" and "Aaahs," and kids pushing and shoving to be closer to him. Kids were five rows deep. I couldn't get to him. Everybody was following him. He was sketching the elderly, the toddlers, all the people around him. He gave the drawings to the children, who were delighted. He'd done the same thing when my boys were little to keep them quiet in a restaurant. They would say "Choo-Choo," and Ilie would draw an entire train with all the details. He would have made a great witness to a crime scene. He would have drawn an image like a photograph.

Ilie wanted to see the apartment where we used to live. Eighteen Chusan Road. He asked our guide, "Do you think we can go upstairs to look?" The guide asked the family if they would mind, and an elderly woman invited us in. The first thing I noticed was a computer on a desk facing the alley, which made no sense to me. A computer in that space felt as if a futuristic time machine had accidentally left behind its contents. The walls were still covered with our green paper, and the curtain that Papa had made still hung over the closet. It was falling apart, but they hadn't bothered to remove it. Looking up, I was mesmerized by the little red flowers. Ed asked, "Don't you want to look at the alley?" I kept staring at the curtain. My whole childhood had been lived behind it to go to the bathroom and to bathe. It was the only privacy I ever had. I couldn't take my eyes off it. I stared and stared. I pointed it out to Ilie. "The curtain's still here."

He said, "Yeah, so it is . . ." but he was looking at the alley.

I said to Ed, "Look at that piece of fabric! Papa made that whole thing. It used to hang all the way down to the ground." Ed looked at it. It didn't mean anything to him. To me, it meant everything.

The family who lived there invited us to stay for dinner. There were five of them, and they were sleeping all over identical to the way we lived. They even put the bed in the same place my parents slept. For a moment, I almost felt my parents standing beside me. It was a shock to the system. I saw Ed and Mitchell beside me, and I swallowed back my brewing tears.

As we were leaving, a man came over to us. He spoke to our guide. He asked if we used to live in the building. He was the houseboy who was always sweeping so he could live in the little alley. He was the kid Mutti used to warn me about, "Don't look. Don't talk to him." Now, he was a sixty-year-old man, but he remembered us as the "little redheaded girl and a little redheaded boy." I pointed to Ilie. "That's the one there, drawing." I asked the guide, "I'd like to take a picture with him." So the man went back and put on a clean shirt, and we took a picture of all of us.

In China, Ed bought every history book he saw about World War II, the Jews in Shanghai, stories written by survivors. He thought I might be interested in them. When he gave them to me, I shoved them to the bottom of our suitcase so he wouldn't read them in front of me. I had no desire to see myself among their pages. Going back to China had rekindled the anger within me once again. I had learned to be angry at an early age, and though I did my best to contain it, a great deal of my life was spent playing out the jack story.

The jack story is this: A man's car breaks down, and he needs a jack. He sees a house far away, and the whole time he's walking toward the house, he's cursing, "Goddamn it, I'm going to have to walk all this way to this damn house, and the person's not even going to open the door, and they won't have a jack, and why am I even bothering to walk?" He curses and predicts all the miserable things that will happen to him. When he gets to the door, an old woman opens it and hands him a jack. Since China, I had lived my life like that cursing man. Angry and convinced that nothing would work out for the best. I expected the worst. I braced myself at all times, never expecting good things to happen.

So I had no desire to read those history books. I knew why I had grown up in the ghettos of Shanghai. I knew what happened to all the other Jews who didn't get on the boat with us. I knew that Hitler was a murderous bastard. I didn't need to do research about the war. I didn't want to read books about it. I didn't need to know what provoked Hitler. I didn't care why the Germans were always followers, why they'd always done exactly what they're told to do. I didn't want to hear that Germans never questioned the leaders. I didn't want to read that the soldiers were good people swayed by a charismatic leader, that the Germans have always been cut and dry, that there is no gray area among Germans, that it's always black and white. I never wanted exposure to an explanation that would make me feel sorry for those soldiers. I didn't want to be presented with an explanation of why I should give my anger another thought, and not in a zillion years would I ever want to see myself among the pictures in those books. But that's exactly where I was. In the pages of those history books. A little girl raising her hand in class. A little girl sitting politely waiting to be called upon by a teacher who never took her home for the weekend. There I was. There I was. There I was.

It made me mad as hell.

BROTHER

The nature of the clothing business had changed. It was going the way of Ed's business, Banana Republic. I was designing for a special kind of woman, but she was disappearing. Women were not dressing that way anymore, and the buyers weren't buying clothes anymore. They were buying deals. "Are you going to take it back when they don't sell at the end of the season? How much markdown money are you going to give me?" It wasn't about fashion anymore, and I didn't like deals. I never took clothes back. That was engraved in stone. I told them it was written in the Torah. Thou shall not take clothes back. Their demands became impossible to meet. I saw the handwriting on the wall. I saw the business heading south.

Stores kept expanding. They weren't run by merchants anymore. The merchants really loved clothing, but they were gone. There were big conglomerates that were bought by other companies, and the companies that bought them paid way too much for them. They had to make their money back, and the only way to do that was through expansion. They kept expanding stores, but the customer base didn't expand. So the slices of the pie had to become smaller. They didn't care how they made money. If they could make more money selling peanuts on the floor, they'd sell peanuts. The whole fashion business turned into something else. It turned away from what I was doing. I didn't have any interest in that market. I didn't have the resources for it. You needed big resources, and I was never that social in the garment business. I did what I had to do, and I went home. I took out buyers once in a while, but I was not part of the scene. I wanted to be an artist, not a salesman.

I was still painting on the weekends. It was a hobby until I said, "I quit. This is it. I don't want this kind of business. That hassle." It took about three days for me to make that decision. Maybe less. There was no transition. People retire with big worries. "What am I going to do when I retire?" I never had that problem. I didn't have to look for things to do. I walked right out of fashion because I knew exactly what I was going to do. I was going to paint.

PART VI

HOLOCAUST MUSEUM

BROTHER

I'd spent my seventieth birthday with Susan, Deborah, and my daughters at the Holocaust Museum in Washington, D.C. It was a moving experience. Before I even entered the museum, they had a hall where they showed a movie explaining the background of the Holocaust. There were tons of children there. High school. Black kids, white kids. Right in front of us, there were a bunch of teenagers, maybe fifteen or sixteen years old, and before the presentation, they were jostling and joking and all over the place, noisy. They sat through the film, and when it was over, there was not a peep out of them. They were demure. They filed out. Something touched them, something had penetrated, and for that alone, it was worth the entire museum. The museum is not for Jews. We know what happened, we were part of it. The museum is for those rowdy teenagers. I was deeply impressed by their reaction.

A curator discovered that Deborah and I had been in the Shanghai ghetto, and she asked if we'd be willing to look at photos to see if we could identify any of the people. We were escorted to the archives, and one of the first photos they showed us was of Deborah at ten years old. They asked if I had any documents and would I mind donating them to the museum. I knew absolutely I had to donate them because I wanted them to be part of the record. They would know how to preserve them. At home, in a suitcase, in a closet, eventually they would disintegrate.

When I returned home, I dug through the closets and found every passport, visa, birth certificate, and pass that had ever touched Mutti's hand. Out of everything Mutti lost in her life, she was able to keep those papers. She had to have them. She couldn't afford to lose them. They were our identity. Without those papers, we didn't exist. Without proof that we were allowed to exist, we would have been slaughtered. Mutti had kept them all. She never let any of them go. Ever. Her entire life. She did not leave them behind in China. She did not leave them in Canada, and she never destroyed them even after Papa died. She remembered the sound of the soldiers demanding, "Papers, papers." She held tightly to our papers, papers. Americans don't know what that is to have the freedom to cross from state border to state border with no identification. It is a miraculous freedom.

Being the eldest and the son, I became the keeper of the documents. I had a suitcase full of them. I had three or four stateless passports myself. Each country had given me a new one. They brought back memories of the first time I traveled to New Jersey without showing any documentation, any proof. I thought it was amazing. That started me thinking visually.

I could see the documents working as a collage using a grid to reflect the size of the passports; space all marked off, to play against it, mostly in black and white with some color, shades of gray. It gave me the opportunity to create a visual composition between the text and the writings and the signatures and the photographs and the symbols. Eagles, there were always eagles; I don't know why, but every country loved the eagle as a symbol of power. Bits and pieces of typewriters. I could use the seals, the stamps. I researched the photos of the stamps, and then, I found Papa's accordion passport. The one that had saved his life, over and over and over again. I used pages from it and began a series of small paintings.

Something broke loose in me. I created twelve small paintings within a month. I wasn't experimenting. I knew exactly what I wanted, so the process didn't take long. These were modern, dark, and structured.

I'd met a curator at a party a year before, a woman who owned a gallery in East Hampton. I'd been introduced as a painter, and she wasn't interested, she had a lot of painters already, landscape artists and such. Still, I decided to get back in touch with her. I told her about the work. I explained that the paintings were based on my father's documents and our time in Shanghai during the Holocaust. She perked up and said, "Don't show them to anyone else. Show them to me first." I showed her the small pieces, all twelve of them. She included them in a group show.

Friends and family came to the opening. It felt better to be recognized as an artist than as a designer. I was doing something that had more substance to it. More heft. More gravitas. I enjoyed designing, but it wasn't something that could last beyond me. I'd seen great designers, people I admired, once they died, their business closed, and they were gone. They were remembered only by fashion people, if at all. They were yesterday's newspaper.

Whether my family loved what I was doing out of support for me or because of their critical judgment, I couldn't tell, but they were there for me. It was a great evening. The gallery sold six of my paintings, ending the night on a very upbeat note. I was encouraged. I decided to start a new series of larger paintings.

I returned to my studio in the Central Park West apartment overlooking the reservoir that Sylvia had scared me into buying so many years before. Every day, I offered up blessings for her wisdom in choosing such a beautiful home where I could create. I spent my days filling bigger canvases, doing variations, exploring different aspects. I wanted a series. I wanted to hit people over the head with them. It took about a year. There was lots of staring at the canvas required. I'd put a mark on it then realize it was not quite right, so I'd stare some more. Staring takes a long time.

Then I went to a show at the Pamela Williams Gallery in Amagansett, New York. After a friend of mine made an introduction, I brought her the photographs of the big paintings. She was impressed enough to give me a one-man show.

It was my first one-man show as a painter. It was well attended, and people were emotionally responsive. They assumed I must have gone through a great emotional catharsis with the paintings. That I must have been haunted by my parents as I worked, but to be honest, I didn't. My parents weren't on my mind as I painted. My mind was on the mechanics of painting. How to create something visually compelling.

My mind was on the logistics. I had to think logically choosing where to put what, to make sense, to do something visually interesting. Painting that series didn't feel like a visitation to me. My father's face became removed from my memories of him. It became a graphic element. My father was not a shy person. He would not have objected to me using his image over and over again. Mutti would not have questioned why she wasn't more a part of the paintings. It was not her way.

I was sad to disappoint the attendees because they wanted a romantic vision of an artist in great turmoil, wrestling with great emotion, but I wasn't tortured emotionally. Like the actor who does a great performance and people weep, but he doesn't have to weep. He's only the conduit. If an artist gets too emotionally involved, it impedes the work. I had to be rational about my passions. I had lived with those documents my entire life. I had moved on, and they got left behind in a suitcase. I wasn't nostalgic about them. They weren't the good old days. They were evidence of what had transpired. They were part of the historical record. I had a sense of responsibility about them. I agreed to be interviewed for Shoah and decided to contribute the documents to the Holocaust Museum in order to tell the story. I had to bear witness. I had to do that. The paintings provided even further evidence of my family's experience. That accordion passport saved our lives, but I didn't attach any metaphysical value to it. Mutti could never release them, but I could. They weren't hard to give away. It was the right thing to do.

SISTER

I told myself ahead of time, I wasn't going to get emotional at the Holocaust Museum. I went there with the intention to look at the exhibits as if they were contemporary art. To figure out what the artist wanted to say. Only I didn't want to know what those images had to say. I tried to look at the exhibits fast, gloss over them, but everybody else was lingering. I focused on the cots and the blankets. Nothing that would sink in. I didn't want to feel sad. I didn't want to be forced to have a feeling. If I couldn't feel, then it wouldn't hurt.

I kept walking, and there was a small exhibit dedicated to the Shanghai ghetto. I glanced at a photo and recognized a kid from my class. That's when I realized I couldn't be too far behind. I wanted to run away, but it was too late. Ilie's daughter, Maris had seen the exhibit, and everyone was headed over.

Like a punch in the gut, I recognized the face staring back at me as my own—my five-year-old self, freckles across her nose, my nose, bruises on her knees, my knees, a bow in her hair, my hair. I couldn't believe it, at first, and then I remembered that moment. That photo in the park before the sword pierced my thigh. There it was. Right on the wall.

I stared at it as if the little girl in the photo was not me. There she was sitting beside two other little kids on a hot day, it was always a hot day, and the three of them were mostly limbs, soft and fleshy, with fair arms and legs just turning lanky, dressed in clean, freshly pressed summer jumpers. At first glance, the photo really did look like three little children caught playing in a park, the trees in full bloom, and the grass under their feet, seated on a rock. Just three little kids from anywhere, living anywhere, like all the other little kids in the whole wide world. Friends playing in a park. I knew better. I knew to look a little closer at our faces. We were five, maybe six or maybe four years old, and already, our eyes were full of worry. We had deep-set eyes, brows heavy with concern. We didn't look away. There was sadness to our expressions that could not be dismissed. Our lips didn't know how to smile. We still wore the plump, smooth cheeks of leftover baby fat, cheeks that would have been pinched by aunts and uncles, grandparents, and visiting family friends had they not all been murdered, gassed, shot. We sat on that rock, the three little kids, and we posed for the Japanese, and we pretended to be happy, but we already looked like the adults we would become. Displaced. Pensive. Self-contained. Two minutes after that photo was taken, I'd been stabbed in the leg.

There were more photos of me. The ones that made it into the history books. Me in the classrooms. I was sitting among boys and girls tucked behind thin, wood tables that functioned as desks, the girls wearing knee-high socks with our skirts, most of the boys in button-up shirts and sweater vests. We had, in front of us, tablets of fresh paper, rulers, and pencil cases. In one photo, our teacher held a pencil in the air, and we mimicked her, lifting our pencils into the air. It was a posed moment that rang so false some of the girls in the photo looked as if they were trying not to laugh. Were we told to pretend to ask a question? Did the Japanese not understand that when a question was asked, you just raised your hand, not your pencil?

Were we receiving a lecture about the value of lead, the scarcity of pencils, and the importance of a finely shaved tip?

When I saw my own face on the wall, it became a reality. I still wasn't going to throw myself on the ground and weep even if other people were crying. I heard a woman say, "I can't believe it." I believed it all right because I knew half the people in the photo. I had no interest in reliving any more of my childhood among those walls but that's when a curator asked us to come to the archives. I begrudgingly put on my glasses. I wanted to flee.

Ilie was inspired by the museum. I was not. I felt it was because of our Jewish heritage that all our suffering had happened. Had we not been Jewish, we wouldn't have lost all of Mutti's family. Papa would not have died at such an early age. Mutti wouldn't have lived such a fearful life. I would have spoken up sooner and not been so painfully shy. Between the Holocaust and the rabbi kicking me out of the temple when Papa died on my lap, I was finished with religion. I had declared myself an atheist years before. Ilie shook his head, "How could you? Knowing what happened!" I told him, "That's why." I didn't want to talk about our visit to the museum. I wanted to shelve it away with the history books Ed kept buying.

P*ART* *VII*

ILLNESS and ED

SISTER

I wanted to return to my life, fundraising in San Francisco and be done with it, but for the entirety of a year, I couldn't keep my balance. Literally. I wasn't actually falling on the ground, but I kept *feeling* as if I would fall at any moment. At first, I thought I was having anxiety attacks and treated it as such. I ended up going to psychiatrists who wanted me to talk about Mutti and Papa. Everyone with the mother and the father discussions! The vertigo got worse when I thought I should be getting better. One doctor wanted to shave the side of my head thinking it could be a brain tumor. I wouldn't let him do it. Ed yelled, "Are you out of your mind! You'd rather die than cut your hair?" I'd inherited Mutti's vanity. My answer was simply yes.

Ed collected *Life* magazines from 1936 to 1972, and he still had every single one of them. He remembered the cover of one, a doctor who had gone to the Congo to study inner-ear problems. He tracked the doctor down. He was coming to New York to give a lecture. The man was ancient and not taking any patients. Ed begged him to use me as a model for his lecture. So there I was, in front of an entire lecture hall full of students, getting poked and prodded and being used as a lab rat. I had scar tissue on my inner ear left by an infection that never healed. The doctor told me it would take two years to heal, and sure enough my problem disappeared after almost two years. But for a year, I thought it possible that I had a brain tumor. It inspired me to throw my next fundraiser for pediatric brain tumor research.

Ellen DeGeneres performed. She'd just publicly come out as a lesbian, and her show had been killed. She was headed back to stand-up comedy and was trying out new material. Over two thousand people bought tickets at Davies Symphony Hall, and Sharon Stone introduced her. She was terrific, just exquisite, and hilarious. Michael Douglas came with his wife, Catherine Zeta Jones, and his father, Kirk Douglas. Danny DeVito and Karl Malden also attended. It was a huge event. I raised a great deal of money for the hospital not knowing that two weeks later, Ed would end up there.

We'd gone to see the Nutcracker ballet, and Ed was in severe pain. It was the year 2000, and they were shutting down the computers for Y2K. Since I had just raised a fortune for the UCSF Pediatric Brain Tumor Department, Dr. Charles Wilson and Dr. Mitch Berger made sure to keep the equipment running so Ed could have all the testing. They even visited us at home to boost Ed's morale. They were like brothers to him. We found out on New Year's Eve. Pancreatic cancer. Ed's first reaction was to look at me and say, "What's going to happen to you?"

He was in the best shape you can imagine. He was never sick. He worked out every single day, we had a gym in the house, and he was religious about it. He was quite disciplined that way. I did research to find people who had survived. I found a Chinese man who had pancreatic cancer and survived for five years. He said his life was hell every day. Even though he survived, he was in constant pain. His wife told me "If you keep strong, it'll give him strength." I took her advice and stayed strong for Ed throughout his treatment. I'd seen Mutti bite at her knuckles my whole life. I knew how to worry in quiet. I had both Eastern European and Chinese backgrounds. I had doubled my stoicism. I was determined not to show fear. I convinced myself it was fine when everyone else knew it was hopeless. My friend, Lois, stayed right by my side as Ed had surgery, and they thought they got it all. I really believed he would pull through. I knew the percentage was low, but I felt I had control over it like I had control of my fundraisers. I knew they would be successful. I knew I could make him well. I had the support of our good friend, Don Fisher, who Ed had worked for at the Gap. Even though Ed wasn't working for the Gap anymore, he was still very close with Don.

Ed had moved on becoming a hired gun first for The Discovery Channel, then for The Nature Company, then for A Pea in the Pod. He consulted for Restoration Hardware and Peet's Coffee, but throughout all those jobs, Ed and Don remained good friends. During Ed's operation, Don and his wife stayed with me, as did my sons and my brother and Lois. I was grateful to have everyone around me, and I thought we had lucked out. We had access to a world-class specialist. Everything was going to be fine.

Although Ed's treatment was at a top hospital, I was frustrated, not getting information about how he was doing. Every time I asked, the response was, "He's in great hands," but Ed wasn't handling the chemo well. While he never lost his hair, his ankles swelled with edema that just didn't make sense. I tried to get answers to my questions, but to no avail. Ilie said, "You need an answer. Go talk to the doctor." I waited at the hospital and followed the doctor out the door. I was assured everything was under control. I pressed, "Then why all the swelling? What's going on with the ankles?" The answer was that it was common, and I needn't worry.

But I *was* worried. Ed was weak and visibly uncomfortable. He was suffering, and though he never complained, I could tell we needed another opinion. There was a doctor in Texas, but I didn't want to take Ed on a commercial jet for fear he would catch something. I called Don and asked if we could pay to use one of the Gap jets. Even though they wanted no payment for this, Ed was insistent that we pay. Mickey Drexler, CEO at that time, made it happen. He was such a busy man, traveling all over the world, still he saw to it that we were on that plane and kept checking on us to make sure we were okay. We met with the top doctor, and instantly after he examined Ed, I wished we'd gone there from day one.

The Texas doctor called to speak with the San Francisco lead doctor covering Ed's case. He felt Ed's treatment needed to be adjusted. The Texas doctor did not get a return call. When finally reached, I asked, "Why haven't you returned his call?" The response was, "Well, there's no sense in me calling him now. We are going to be at the same convention, and I will bump into him anyway. I'll talk to him there." Three weeks went by, and Ed's treatments had not been adjusted in any way. The edema kept coming back. Ed was miserable, drugged out, and dying. I just about broke down the San Francisco doctor's door to no avail. The doctor couldn't be found. Ed passed away without the knowledge or compassion of his doctor. In fact, I had to convey the news that he was gone.

My grief hid neatly behind my anger. The day after the funeral, I called Don and told him "I'm not letting this ride. I can't bring him back, but I can say something." I wrote a very strong letter with the help of my sons because I didn't want to get too emotional. I wanted to stick to the facts and not sound like a grieving housewife. I wanted to hand deliver the letter to the head of the hospital. I asked my two sons to come with me. I didn't want to go alone.

It was impossible to get an appointment with this man. It seemed that the only people who got to see him were those writing checks. I called, but was turned away. I phoned Don one more time asking for his help. He said, "Tell them you're calling at my suggestion." That worked.

I knew when we walked in this man thought I would be delivering a check. The three of us sat in front of him and formalities were exchanged. I took a tranquilizer before because I feared I'd jump out of my skin if I didn't. I gave him the letter and made sure he read it in front of us. I had kept a diary of every medication Ed took, the reactions from the medicine, the doctor's reactions, the reactions from me, what happened to Ed and documented every instance when the lead doctor was too busy to help. I had everything logged by the date. He read it and was shocked. I said, "I wanted you to see I'm not a hysterical widow. I have no intention of suing, but I wanted you to meet my two sons who have been robbed of their father. I wanted to be here when you read the letter to make sure you read it. I've accomplished it, so thank you for seeing me." Then we left.

The next morning, the lead doctor called me, frantic, asking if we could meet. I refused. The next comment was so naive, "In the letter you said I didn't get back to you for four weeks. That's wrong. It was three weeks." I hung up. Don received a call from the doctor blaming the hospital for the preoccupation with writing grants and attending conventions, making it difficult to see patients or supervise staff. Don called me to explain the situation. I called the head of the hospital and said, "I stand corrected. I've been informed by your chair that my husband's lead doctor would've loved to help him, but was kept busy in the hospital and was prevented from seeing patients." Needless to say, that did the trick.

It didn't bring him back, and my anger was overwhelming. Ed had been taken in his prime. I felt cheated. It was the final injustice, losing Ed before we'd had the chance to grow old together. I wanted someone to pay. I wanted to start a movement that would bring compassion back to medicine. I wanted to force doctors to learn compassion in school. The doctors were so familiar with death. They'd hardened themselves against the individuality of each patient. I understood it. I'd done the same thing in China. I'd grown numb to death, but now that I'd seen that same coldness expressed in an American hospital, I wanted compassion. I wanted to train physicians to remain hopeful. Why not take a different approach? Why treat the critically ill as if they were already dead? How could a patient have any hope left?

I preferred the days when patients were not told they were dying. Mutti wasn't told she was dying. We were told. They took the family aside and told us the truth. The patient had a choice then. They could ask, "Am I going to live?" The family could decide what was best for their loved one. Now, the doctors don't give you that option. They seal your fate under the guise of "we need to tell the patient the truth." You hear those words, and that becomes the fact of the matter. Hope falls by the wayside.

I wanted to go to the papers. I actually already had a committee in place when I spoke to my lawyer. He told me, "Bear in mind, if you become a spokesperson, you will be reliving it each time."

At first, I said, "I don't care. If I can help other people that's what I want to do."

Then Ilie put it in terms I better understood: the language of film. My brother said, "Do you really want to be the Norma Rae of cancer?"

I did not want to be the Norma Rae of cancer.

I resolved myself to grieving. I never showed emotion, I had never cried in front of Ed. There was one moment, when I had weakened and gotten teary, and he'd encouraged me, "It's healthy to cry." I had quickly straightened myself up. I felt I had to be so strong for him. Now, that strength was gone. I couldn't tell my children how devastated I was, so I found a psychiatrist, a woman. I called her at night and cried over the phone.

All those years with Ed, I should have been more affectionate.

I was wracked with guilt, enormous amounts of guilt. I wish I did this. I wish I did that. I began to idolize him. He became the perfect man. No one else could possibly measure up. Then I wanted closure. What would he have wanted for me after he passed away? We never talked about the what-if, and that was a mistake. A widowed friend of mine had gone to Paris, had started traveling all over the world to honor the request of her dying husband. I had no idea what Ed would want me to do.

I'd spent every moment of my life being cared for by someone else. Mutti had taken care of me. Ed had taken care of me. Becoming a widow ... some women say it feels like freedom, but for me, it was terribly confusing. I had a brand new set of wings, and I didn't know what to do with them. All the decisions were now my decisions. My life was now completely my life. I'd never had to think about what I wanted my life to be. I'd never had any real choices about it. I felt incredibly burdened. I wanted to turn to Ed and ask, "Do you want me to miss you forever? Do you want me to meet someone else? Should I quit fundraising?" He wasn't there to answer.

The only thing I knew how to do was move. I had to get out of that gigantic house that had been such a joy to build, had seemed like the resolution of my deprivation, the house that became my haven. Now, it felt empty and barren, and it scared me to be inside it at night by myself. I packed my things and moved and moved and moved and moved once more finding myself, ironically, in a Nob Hill apartment overlooking Chinatown. I even filled the apartment with Chinese art, vases, and artifacts. Without being consciously aware of my decision, I had, in some sense, finally come full circle.

John, the cheating Marine from my teen years, waltzed back into my life. Or tried to. One visit to San Francisco put an end to that fantasy. In my mind, he'd always been that strapping young soldier in a uniform. Once I saw him standing in front of me, that fantasy was dispelled. His youth had faded leaving no trace of the boy I once loved. He'd married a woman from Shanghai, the daughter of the rabbi who married my parents. He'd married her on the same day of the same month, different year that I'd married Ed. In other words, we had the same wedding anniversary. He claimed it was all coincidence, that he'd forgotten my background, my wedding date, it was all serendipity. I didn't buy it. I was cured of my old regrets, albeit decades too late. Why had I wasted so much energy wondering what could have been?

I returned to China once again, this time taking my friends and revealing to them the truth of my background, my history. I took them back to Chusan Road, and just as we got out of the car, another car pulled up. There were two Chinese people getting out, and they spoke perfect English. The woman in the cab asked if she could help us, if we were lost. I explained to her that I'd grown up in the building and pointed to the window where Ilie had been sitting when the bombs dropped. She said, "My parents live next door. The apartments are identical if you'd like to see inside."

We walked up those rickety stairs to meet her mother who was ninety years old. She remembered me immediately, and her daughter began to translate for us. "There was a couple with a little redheaded boy and girl, and the little girl was not allowed to play with you." The daughter stopped, realizing what she had said, and instantly, we knew one another again. The daughter was my hopscotch friend, the little girl I'd sneak out to play with before Mutti would notice I was gone. We were both beside ourselves with shock. My friends burst into tears.

The trip, the resolution with John, letting go of the house, were these changes enough to finally let go of my past, to concentrate not on a distant, hoped-for future, but instead to live in the now, the now being all I will ever have? Could I accept that life had taken a turn for the better and blessed me with good fortune? What was the final piece of the puzzle? What action would finally free me? How many more fundraisers would I have to throw before I could finally say, "It's enough. I don't owe anyone else for my survival. There's no one else to pay back."

That was it. That was it. I had to be willing to give it all away and start entirely over. I was willing. I am willing. I willed myself to say:

Give me the final bill. I'm done.

P_{ART} *VIII*

ACCEPTANCE AND LEGACY

BROTHER

It ends with my sister and me. We leave behind, or we hope we do, some sort of legacy. Deborah will leave behind her a legacy of philanthropy, having raised millions for various organizations in San Francisco. She became a woman our parents would not have recognized. Long gone was the little girl from Shanghai who was too scared to leave Mutti's side. With Ed gone and her sons married with children of their own, Deborah blossomed. Her gumption came bubbling to the surface. She quickly made up for lost time! She took the position of deputy chief of protocol for the city, greeting and hosting dignitaries from all over the world. She was appointed to the San Francisco Public Library commission overseeing the policymaking for dozens of libraries, and then the mayor gave her a key to the city for all the work she'd done. I'd never been more proud.

And me? Hopefully, my clothes made some women very happy. Susan and I were at the Whitney Museum, and there was a woman wearing a coat of mine. Knee length, A-line, the top was black with a waistline that had a yellow band, and the bottom was purple. The collar was yellow and black to repeat the colors in the coat. Susan went to her and said, "That's a great coat you're wearing." The woman said, "I love it." "You want to meet the designer?" The woman was thrilled. She had lost the label in the coat, so I borrowed a black pen, and I signed my name on the lining. Nothing she saw at the museum excited her as much as meeting the designer of the coat. The coats themselves have lives beyond me.

But who remembers even great designers? Who remembers their name ten years after they've died? It's all ephemeral. Gone. Nothing. Artists have a chance at immortality. A very faint chance, but a chance. I wanted to do something. To leave a legacy behind me. I knew if I could leave some art behind, I might have a chance of living longer. While designing a coat and painting a picture may be an expression of the same impulse to create, the artist has a better chance at immortality, albeit a slim one. Long after the coat has turned into a schmatte, becoming threadbare, the lining disintegrating, the buttons falling off, the painting is still there, hopefully hanging on someone's wall, and if you are lucky, in a museum. I want to be in the latter group. If there was anything that growing up in Shanghai taught me, it was that life is transitory, and you need to choose very carefully what is important to you. Were there any other lessons to be learned from that suffering? Any other redeeming insight that guided my choices?

Does it matter? What I choose to love is painting and running around the reservoir, though these days it is mostly walking, and playing tennis. I love my daughters, Maris and Darin, both of them so gifted, both of them visual artists. Maris won a prestigious graphic-design competition and went on to positions at Rolling Stone magazine and even worked for Jim Henson's company with The Muppets.

Darin, a talented sculptor, designed the interactive programs for the children's museum in Palo Alto, California. She created the large sculpture that adorns the entrance and became, like my sister did at one point, a successful interior designer.

I feel blessed to still have Deborah in my life, to have found Susan, for my grandchildren, one named after Charles Jordan to honor the man who plucked me out of poverty and granted me a new life. I'm grateful I had so many happy years with Sylvia. The lessons of the Shanghai years have been internalized. I look at life with equanimity. Most days I am at my easel, some days there is inspiration and some days, not so much. Either way, I'm here, and I feel great. Maybe that's the key to survival. Happiness with the mundane.

As I sit with my morning coffee staring out of my window facing Central Park, am I thinking how lucky I am to be alive? No. I am thinking that the windows need washing.

SISTER

I never wanted to tell this story. My childhood in China, I detested. I spent the entirety of my life avoiding those memories, putting the past behind me, trying to forget, trying to compensate for what was lost. To willingly self-identify as a survivor, that was something I would never, ever do. It was my secret. I meant to take it with me to my grave.

But when Ed died, I found strength inside myself I never knew existed. I have come to understand that the tragedies I experienced forged my character and fueled me to reach out in the only way I knew to help: by raising money to combat diseases. It was a way to give back without giving too much of myself. It allowed me a level of participation without intimacy. I wasn't yet brave enough to claim my heritage.

Now, my children have children, and their lives are good. Mark became the lead meteorologist of the Bay Area. Mitchell founded a telemedicine-consulting company called MEDamorphous and now works as the vice president for another company in the same industry. Between the two sons, I have five grandchildren, four girls and one boy.

Those years in China are almost forgotten. They will be entirely forgotten if I don't pass my story to them. To have survived and to have thrived, that is a tribute to my parents, yes, but to let their lives go unrecorded, for our great-grandchildren never to know their history, that would be my fault. It's not a burden I want to carry. I tell this story, knowing that the old resentments, the poverty and the hatred and the deaths of so many I loved did not destroy me, but instead, inspired me.

There are days, yes, when I stand in utter amazement at the trajectory of my life almost as if I'm hovering over myself and watching a poor, little girl dressed in an Army blanket having dinner with King Carlos of Spain or meeting President Clinton's plane at the airport or attending one of Ilie's opening nights. I still feel as if I might need to beg for food. I have to pinch myself to come back into my own skin. The euphoria that accompanies such moments finds its counterpoint in a lingering fear.

Revisiting these memories has conjured terror. Reading the words on the page feels like reading someone else's story, a novel. I have to remind myself it's a memoir. I empathize with my parent's struggle. I root for my brother's successes. But me? I never count myself into the equation. I have to now. I speak about my past, and suddenly, my life makes more sense.

I think about my sons, that it's not just about me, and I have tried too long to protect them from the ugliness of my childhood at the cost of my own truth. I finally push myself past the old hurts in a way I have never done. Not with my brother, not with my children, not even in the privacy of a therapist's office. My God, the years I spent asking "why me?" or "why us?" and now, I see that I robbed myself of happiness. I couldn't stop to enjoy my own life. Those days are over.

I am changed by telling my story. This is a freedom I've never felt before. There's nothing left to hide, and honestly, I wasn't very good at it anyway. I was hiding in plain sight. It's a great relief to stop pretending, to stop holding in and holding back. My past has been like all those old passports and visas and papers Mutti carried around. Weighty and no longer necessary. I am no longer on the streets begging. It's okay to enjoy life. It's okay to chase those old dreams.

I won't sit idle. There's still too much work to be done. Tackling homelessness, that's on my list. Everyone deserves to have a roof over their heads. I would be very proud of myself if I could make an impact with the homeless situation in America.

Expressing myself creatively has also become extremely important. I finally found my voice, and I want to use it to inspire others. There are so many older people who have lived amazing lives and who have great wisdom and mentoring skills that the younger generations need. Life isn't over for them, and their voices need to be heard by a larger, mainstream audience. I want to find a way to do more than fund-raise. I want to heart-raise and mind-raise and ambition-raise.

The possibilities are endless.